Awakening to Educational Supervision

Awakening to Educational Supervision

A Mindfulness-Based Approach to Coaching and Supporting Teachers

Steve Haberlin, PhD
University of Central Florida

ROWMAN & LITTLEFIELD
Lanham • Boulder • New York • London

Executive Acquisitions Editor: Nathan Davidson
Assistant Acquisitions Editor: Hollis Peterson
Sales and Marketing Inquiries: textbooks@rowman.com

Published by Rowman & Littlefield
An imprint of The Rowman & Littlefield Publishing Group, Inc.
4501 Forbes Boulevard, Suite 200, Lanham, Maryland 20706
www.rowman.com

86–90 Paul Street, London EC2A 4NE

Copyright © 2024 by Steve Haberlin

All rights reserved. No part of this book may be reproduced in any form or by any electronic or mechanical means, including information storage and retrieval systems, without written permission from the publisher, except by a reviewer who may quote passages in a review.

British Library Cataloguing in Publication Information Available

Library of Congress Cataloging-in-Publication Data

Names: Haberlin, Steve, 1972– author.
Title: Awakening to educational supervision : a mindfulness-based approach to coaching and supporting teachers / Steve Haberlin.
Description: Lanham, Maryland : Rowman & Littlefield, 2024. | Includes bibliographical references and index.
Identifiers: LCCN 2023030235 (print) | LCCN 2023030236 (ebook) | ISBN 9781538141175 (cloth) | ISBN 9781538141182 (paperback) | ISBN 9781538141199 (epub)
Subjects: LCSH: School personnel management—United States. | Teacher-administrator relationships—United States. | Teachers—Rating of—Methodology. | Teaching—Evaluation—Methodology. | Mindfulness (Psychology)
Classification: LCC LB2831.58 .H34 2024 (print) | LCC LB2831.58 (ebook) | DDC 371.2/010973—dc23/eng/20230814
LC record available at https://lccn.loc.gov/2023030235
LC ebook record available at https://lccn.loc.gov/2023030236

Contents

Foreword by Stephen Gordon	ix
Preface	xi
Acknowledgments	xv

1 Mindfulness and Its Relevance to Educational Supervision — 1

    Defining Mindfulness — 1
    Historical Roots of Mindfulness — 2
    Scientific Benefits of Mindfulness — 6
    Mindfulness's Relevance to Educational Supervision — 8
    Mindfulness Moment — 9
    The Structure of This Book: Nine Attitudes of Mindfulness — 10
    What to Expect in This Book — 10

2 A Brief History of Supervision and Overview of Supervision Models (and Where Mindfulness-Based Supervision Fits In) — 15

    Defining Supervision — 15
    A Historical Snapshot of Supervision — 16
    Evolving Views of Supervision — 18
    The Current State of Supervision — 19
    How Can Mindfulness Help the Field of Supervision? — 20
    The Clinical Supervision Model — 20
    The Convergence of Mindfulness and the Clinical Supervision Cycle — 22
    A Mindful Moment — 26
    What's Next? — 28

3	**Developing a Personal Mindfulness Meditation Practice**	**29**
	What Exactly Is Meditation?	29
	Choosing a Mindfulness Meditation Method	31
	Experimentation With Meditation Methods	31
	How Do You Know Your Meditation Is Working?	32
	A Mindfulness-Based Meditation Method: Vipassana	34
	What's Next?	35
4	**Presence in Supervision**	**37**
	Presence in Educational Supervision	38
	Cultivating Presence During the Clinical Supervision Cycle	39
	Presence in Leadership (Six Response Skills)	40
	A Mindful Moment	41
	Mindfulness-Based Practices to Develop Presence	42
	What's Next?	46
5	**Beginner's Mind in Supervision**	**47**
	Beginner's Mind and Educational Supervision	48
	Cultivating Beginner's Mind During the Clinical Supervision Cycle	49
	Beginner's Mind and the Immediate Response Skills	50
	A Mindful Moment	51
	Mindfulness-Based Strategies to Cultivate Beginner's Mind	51
	Example of Beginner's Mind Informing the Clinical Cycle	55
	What's Next?	56
6	**Patience and Trust in Supervision**	**57**
	Patience in Educational Supervision	58
	Trust and Intuition	59
	Intuition and Supervision	61
	Cultivating Patience and Trust During the Clinical Supervision Cycle	62
	Patience and Trust and the Immediate Response Skills	63
	Mindfulness-Based Practices to Encourage Patience and Trust	64
	Example of Patience and Trust (Intuition) Informing the Clinical Cycle	69
	What's Next?	70
7	**Letting Go and Non-Striving as a Supervisor**	**71**
	Letting Go and Non-Striving in Educational Supervision	74
	What's in Your Supervision Backpack?	74

	Cultivating Letting Go and Non-Striving During the Clinical Supervision Cycle	76
	Letting Go and the Immediate Response Skills	77
	Mindfulness-Based Practices for Letting Go	77
	Example of Letting Go and Non-Striving in Supervision	79
	What's Next?	80
8	**Acceptance and Non-Judgment in Supervision**	**81**
	Acceptance and Non-Judgment in Educational Supervision	82
	Cultivating Acceptance and Non-Judgment During the Clinical Supervision Cycle	83
	Mindfulness-Based Strategies to Cultivate Acceptance and Non-Judgment	85
	What's Next?	86
9	**Gratitude and Generosity (Yes, in Supervision)**	**87**
	Gratitude and Generosity in Educational Supervision	89
	Cultivating Gratitude and Generosity during the Clinical Supervision Cycle	89
	Mindfulness-Based Strategies to Cultivate Gratitude and Generosity	91
	Example of Gratitude and Generosity Informing the Clinical Cycle	93
	What's Next?	94
10	**Mindfulness-Informed Educational Leadership: Moving Toward a More Inclusive Approach to Supervision**	**95**
	Embodied Mindfulness as a Tool for Critical Self-Reflection	96
	The Body and Bias	97
	The Inner Work of Culturally Responsive Supervision	98
	Tonglen: Advanced Meditation for Inclusive Educational Leadership	101
	Final Thoughts on Mindfulness-Based Supervision	104
Resources		105
References		109
Index		117
About the Author		123

Foreword

I am familiar with Steve Haberlin's scholarship because of our common interest in the field of supervision and his presentations at meetings of the Council of Professors of Instructional Supervision (COPIS), a group to which we both belong. It was at a COPIS meeting that I first heard Dr. Haberlin present on what to me (and many other members of the council) was a new area of exploration: the connection between mindfulness and educational supervision.

Based on both his experience and scholarship, Haberlin is the right person to write this book. He has practiced mindfulness throughout his career as an educator, utilized it as a supervisor, explored its relationship to supervision in his doctoral research, presented on that relationship at national conferences, and written about it in scholarly publications. Through this book, Haberlin shares powerful ideas and useful practices on the intersection of mindfulness and supervision, relevant for those who supervise pre-service and in-service teachers. Although mindfulness is used in many schools by teachers working with students, and used by some supervisors working with teachers, it generally is not part of supervisory practice, and in large part is absent from supervision scholarship. Given the significant potential of connecting mindfulness with supervision, a well-written book on this topic is needed, and with this publication Haberlin meets that need.

Early in this work, Haberlin defines both mindfulness and supervision and provides a brief history of both. He then makes the case for practicing mindfulness within the context of supervision, especially within clinical supervision, which includes a pre-conference, classroom observation, and post-conference. The reader who is not familiar with mindfulness meditation will appreciate chapter 3, which provides a full explanation of meditation as well as methods for experimenting with and checking one's progress with meditation and its effects. Chapter 4, another foundational chapter, describes *presence*, the state we enter through mindfulness, and the need for presence in supervision. Haberlin shares ideas for fostering presence in each stage of the clinical supervision cycle.

After creating a firm foundation for mindfulness in supervision, Haberlin spends several chapters discussing the nine attitudes of mindfulness: beginner's mind, patience and trust, letting go and non-striving, acceptance and non-judgment, gratitude and generosity. I think the reader will appreciate the way he presents the material in these chapters: first an explanation of the attitude, then a rationale for incorporating the attitude in supervision, then specific methods for infusing the attitude with mindfulness in general and clinical supervision in particular.

The last chapter of the book, on mindfulness-informed, inclusive supervision, addresses another critical topic. In this chapter, Haberlin artfully connects the nine attitudes of mindfulness to culturally responsive supervision. Discussions and exercises on embodied mindfulness as a tool for critical self-reflection and the inner work of culturally responsive supervision are especially helpful. For readers interested in learning more about mindfulness and meditation, near the end of the book Haberlin suggests other books, websites, centers, teachers, and apps to explore.

I consider this book to be of great value for a number of reasons. It makes a strong case to include mindfulness in educational supervision. This book will help supervisors who have not used mindfulness in their work to better understand it and to incorporate it in their practice. This work firmly establishes mindfulness as part of the supervision literature and, hopefully, as part of graduate work for those preparing to be supervisors. Finally, this book opens a path for future research on mindfulness as an aspect of educational supervision.

Stephen P. Gordon
Distinguished Professor Emeritus
Texas State University

Preface

My interest in mindfulness as an approach to enhance educational supervision began in 2018, when working as a graduate assistant and completing my PhD dissertation. At the time, I was supervising about 12 to 20 student teachers per semester, trying to figure out how to best coach and prepare them to inherit their own classrooms while handling my own workload and stress as an impoverished doctoral student.

I had been meditating since my mid-20s (I was in my 40s when I returned to graduate school) and had done a small amount of research, investigating mindfulness practices with elementary students that I taught. Instinctively, I knew mindfulness could benefit all facets of education, including preparing teachers; but driven to know more and expand the boundaries of the field, I committed to the topic as the subject of my dissertation.

During that time, I experimented with a variety of mindfulness-based methods in my own supervision practice, finding it extremely helpful. For instance, when I arrived at a partnership school to meet with or observe the student teachers, I normally felt frazzled and rushed. Nevertheless, in my new "mindfulness supervisor" mode, I intentionally slowed my steps, practicing a form of walking meditation as I made my way to a classroom. I became aware of my breath as each shoe met the shiny, tile hallways of the school. Within minutes I felt more grounded, more present.

When sitting in my office (a crowded room in the back of the school's media center, where the students did the morning news show) and no one was around, I purposely paused, closed my eyes, and practiced a brief mindfulness meditation. With each breath, my shoulders seemed to drop a bit, my muscles relaxing from what typically felt like a constant stream of tension. When I did this before a student teacher came to conference with me, it cleared my mind and allowed me somehow to be more present. I was no longer thinking of the million things I had to do as a doctoral student/instructional supervisor/father/spouse/(fill in the blank). I was actually "there" when the student teacher described their upcoming observation lesson, debriefed after the lesson, or just shared how their internship was going. I also used my breath as an anchor during classroom observations, and it helped me to be more present, collecting evidence and spotting teachable moments. I was much more zoomed into the experience. My real-time thoughts and feelings of mindfulness-based supervision were captured in a series of journal entries, such as this one:

> *Mind racing—just a few minutes before first conference with intern. I stop remember to focus on the breath. I feel calmer, clearer. I feel my job is to first connect with the intern; check on their well-being, their state of mind. Then proceed to instructional planning support. I hear the sound of the heater above. My hands feel cold from outside. I wonder how the interns are doing now that they are in the school five days per week.*
> *Breath . . . out.*
> *Breath . . . out.*

In time, I also experienced more of a flow state when supervising. I was able to be more open, to be more responsive from a place of calm as opposed to reactive, from a place of stress. It wasn't that I no longer experienced the stress of my role but rather that I had the tools (walking meditation, mindfulness meditation) to better manage that stress. Situations that came up, fires I had to put out at the school, didn't throw me for as much of a loop.

Another side effect of trying to be more present as I worked with student teachers was (and this is difficult to capture empirically) that I just felt more in tune with them, more sensitive to their emotional journeys as they strove to become classroom teachers. For example, I journaled this after visiting a student teacher:

> *Her face is tight, tense. Her eyes a bit watery. I wondered what she is thinking, feeling? Her voice seems shaky as she speaks to the students.*

With this heightened awareness, I was in a better position to provide support to this student teacher, which included a follow-up visit later in the day and a conversation.

Over the years I have presented these ideas on mindfulness-enhanced supervision to colleagues in the field, including making several presentations at the Council of Professors of Instructional Supervision (COPIS) annual conference and publishing an article in the group's academic publication, *The Journal of Educational Supervision*. My ideas have received a mainly positive reception (perhaps a few strange looks at times), and supervision scholars, including a number whose work has laid the very foundation for this work to be even possible, have been supportive and helpful in their feedback. However, I think these ideas can go further, can be experimented with more and utilized more in the field. I wholeheartedly believe that mindfulness-based practices—increasing present-moment awareness—can greatly benefit the current state of educational supervision. Hence, the reason I am writing this book: I want to deepen exploration of these ideas and directly share specific strategies that principals, university supervisors, mentor teachers, and others involved in the preparation and coaching of teachers can apply immediately in their practice. Currently, as I write this book, the field of supervision struggles with a number of challenges, from being respected as a field to embracing more culturally responsive approaches to help marginalized teachers and students in schools across the country. The COVID-19 pandemic, which drastically impacted schools, magnified many of the problems inherent in today's education system. It did the same with the systems, models, and methods used to supervise teachers—it revealed deeply ingrained issues that need immediate addressing. Mindfulness is all about living and teaching fully from the present moment, where we have the most and only power to change things. The time is *now*.

With a Peaceful Heart,
Steve Haberlin, PhD

Acknowledgments

First and foremost, I would like to thank my family, including my spouse, Fon, who provides unrelentless support, guidance, common sense, and inspiration.

I would also like to acknowledge my friend and colleague, Ian Mette, who arrived at the perfect time in my academic career. You have been an outstanding example, mentor, fellow philosopher, collaborative academic, and voice of reason.

I also wish to thank the following reviewers whose thoughtful comments and expertise guided my writing and revisions for the development of this book:

Pamela Angelle, *The University of Tennessee*
Kevin Badgett, *University of Texas Permian Basin*
Lisa Baylis, *Esquimalt High School*
Richard Bernato, *St. John's University*
Michelle Boettcher, *Clemson University*
Allison Borden, *University of New Mexico*
Mary Brabeck, *New York University*
Brandon Butler, *Old Dominion University*
James Cates, *Purdue Fort Wayne*
Heather Cato, *Coastal Carolina*
Amie Cieminski, *University of Northern Colorado*
Krista Clancy, *Wayne State University*
Dale Cox, *Utah Valley University*
Benjamin Creed, *Northern Illinois University*
Laurie Elish-Piper, *Northern Illinois University*
Steven Emerson, *Concordia University–St. Paul*
Fenwick English, *Ball State University*
Mary Derrington, *University of Tennessee*
Stephen Gordon, *Texas State University*
Sonya Hayes, *The University of Tennessee*
Frank Hernandez, *Southern Methodist University*
W. Kyle Ingle, *University of Louisville*

Patrick Jenlink, *Stephen F. Austin State University*
Jennifer Jones, *University of Texas at Tyler*
Leslie Lewis, *Clemson University*
James Martinez, *University of Tennessee*
Ian Mette, *University of Maine*
John Miller
Lauren Misiaszek, *Beijing Normal University*
Thomas Morgan, *University of Northern Colorado*
Isabel Nunez, *Purdue University Fort Wayne*
Marilynn Quick, *Ball State University*
Elizabeth Reilly, *Loyola Marymount University*
Dylan Rust, *Northern Arizona University*
Phillip Saisa, *Fitchburg State University*
Wayne Serebrin, *University of Manitoba*
Robert Smith, *George Mason University*
Rolf Straubhaar, *Texas State University*
Kathy Sobolewski, *Charleston Southern University*
Kevin Stockbridge, *Chapman University*
Rolf Straubhaar, *Texas State University*
Megan Sweet, *Leadership Public Schools*
Richard Tomko, *Manhattan College*
Trenia Walker, *University of New Mexico*
Deran Whitney, *Shenandoah University*
Steven Witt, *Department of Graduate Education*
Rebecca Wylie, *University of South Florida*
Sally Zepeda, *University of Georgia*
Aidong Zhang, *Louisiana State University Shreveport*

Finally, I would like to express appreciation to the members of the Council of Professors of Instructional Supervision (COPIS) for welcoming me in as a graduate student and continuing to support my ideas on mindfulness-based supervision.

Chapter One

Mindfulness and Its Relevance to Educational Supervision

DEFINING MINDFULNESS

Mindfulness is a psychological trait or quality of awareness or consciousness (Neale, 2017). A commonly used definition for mindfulness is "the awareness that emerges through paying attention on purpose, in the present moment, and non-judgmentally to the unfolding of experience moment by moment" (Kabat-Zinn, 2003, p. 145). Definitions of mindfulness often emphasize the strengthening of focus, or "refining our capacities for paying attention, for sustained and penetrative awareness, and for emergent insight that is beyond thought but that can be articulated through thought" (Segal, Williams & Teasdale, 2002, p. 8). However, popular definitions often neglect the significance of insight, instead settling on the notion of mindfulness simply being clear, present-moment awareness. While not well-documented, mindfulness provides two key skills: *recognition* and *choice*. These skills enable one to override past, habitual conditioning and "provides an opportunity for more constructive choices about how one relates to external or internal stimuli in the moment" (Neale, 2017, p. 18). Similarly, Salzberg's (2017) definition of mindfulness emphasizes the benefit of non-reactivity and choice when she writes: "It is a quality of awareness in which we are not reacting with grasping, aversion, or delusion. We feel the pleasure, we feel the pain, we experience the neutrality, but we are practicing mindfulness of them rather than being lost in one of these habitual reactions" (p. 38). Another way of understanding mindfulness might be to consider its opposite, or mindlessness, where "we all wear mental blinders, based on past experiences and assumptions without realizing it, cruising on autopilot" (Larrivee, 2012, p. 132). The difficulty in explaining mindfulness lies in that it is something that you already experienced but just needs to be rediscovered and enhanced rather than "created." The practice of mindfulness assists us in dealing with the constant traffic of thoughts in our mind, the wandering mind, or what is also known now in neuroscience as our default network. Mindfulness training helps us "grow and flex what we might call our response muscle" (Hall, 2013, p. 14), the state of mind where we observe and witness and move beyond conditioned responses and negative reactivity that no longer serve us, including within the realm of educational supervision. This element of choice within mindfulness is vital in understanding the role and reason to become more mindful. What's the point in becoming more aware, recognizing more of what's happening, if you don't do anything about it, if you don't make new choices and cultivate new responses? Later in the book we will explore how this factors into various supervision roles and practices.

To help understand mindfulness, try this simple action: Take your hand and wave it across your body. Do it again, a little faster. It probably felt rushed, haphazard. Now, take the same hand and move it across your body slowly, with intention and complete awareness. Do it again, slower, watching your hand as it passes (saying, "I am a Jedi, like my father before"—well, you don't have to really say that to get the point). You might have noticed there was a certain grace when you moved the hand slower. You might have felt a tension in the arm or hand. You might have noticed the space around you more. This is an example of mindfulness. Same movement, different experience.

Depending on one's approach, educational supervision might have become more or less mindful. Perhaps after years of being on the job, school leaders might start operating on autopilot, with mental blinders after years of working with teachers or other educators. One's educational leadership style might have become lost in a reactivity cycle, one where leaders are no longer recognizing or, perhaps, not consciously choosing new responses that truly serve teachers, students, and parents. Mindfulness, or intentional, present-centered awareness, could be the key to remedying this situation.

HISTORICAL ROOTS OF MINDFULNESS

Mindfulness as a form of meditation originated within the Buddhism tradition of India about 500 BCE (Neale, 2017). References to mindfulness can be found in early teachings in a 10,000-word text known as the *Mahasatipatthana Sutra*, which details the *Four Foundations of Mindfulness* (Nisker, 1998; Tremmel, 1993). The term "mindfulness" is a translation of the Sanskrit word *sati* and the Pali word *smrit*, which means "to remember" (Gethin, 2011; Neale, 2017, p. 17). To gain appreciation for mindfulness and understand its contextual roots, one must have some background on Buddhism and Buddhist thought. Buddhism is an ancient, world religion but also framed as practical philosophy and the first working psychology (Neale, 2017). Upon reaching enlightenment, or an awakened state to the nature of reality, the Buddha posited the Four Noble Truths, a framework that outlined the symptoms, causes, and treatment of human suffering. The following interpretation of the Noble Truths is based on work of Western contemplative psychotherapists (Lozzio, 2012, 2015; Neale, 2017). Briefly summarized, the Four Noble Truths are:

1. All life is prone to suffering (sometimes translated as a dissatisfaction), for example: disease, aging, and death. Conditioned reactions "leave the mind and body poisoned by stress instincts and traumatic habits" (Neale, 2017, p. 18).
2. This suffering is caused by an unconscious chain of 12 casually linked neuropsychological processes known as dependent origination.
3. Since this suffering is self-created and self-perpetuated, people can break links in this chain, thus causing the cessation of suffering and achieving psychological liberation, or nirvana.
4. The comprehensive approach for achieving liberation is called the Eightfold Path (realistic view, realistic intention, harmonious lifestyle, truthful speech, proper livelihood, joyous effort, sustained mindfulness, and concentration).

These eight practices can be condensed into three trainings: wisdom, meditation, and ethics, each designed to counteract the reactive stress cycle described in step two of the Noble Truths. The three trainings work synergistically; for instance, living an ethical lifestyle reduces mental afflictions and promotes healthier mind states conducive to meditation and the clarity needed for insight. It should be noted that mindfulness is *only one-third of the Buddhist training or approach*. The West's overemphasis on mindfulness over these other areas, the reduction of mindfulness to a mere stress-reduction technique, and mass-marketing of mindfulness as a panacea has led to the term "McMindfulness" (Purser, 2019; Neale, 2011, 2012).

Four Foundations of Mindfulness

The Eightfold Path of Buddhism is complemented by a practical framework called the Four Foundations of Mindfulness (see table 1.1). "The aim of this meditative pedagogy is to systematically strengthen one's attention by applying it to four discrete domains of experience in order to refine the mind's natural capacity for insight (wisdom) and behavior change (ethics)" (Neale, 2017,

Table 1.1. **Four Foundations of Mindfulness**

Mindfulness Foundation	Description
Mindfulness of Body	Foundation for other mindfulness practices
	Generally involves focusing on the breath to develop calm awareness
Mindfulness of Sensations	Becoming familiar with feelings and the instinct to attach or push away from experience
Mindfulness of Mind	Becoming attuned to the thoughts and mental states
Mindfulness of Realities	Awareness of natural phenomena

p. 20). The four foundational domains are mindfulness of (1) body, (2) sensations, (3) mind, and (4) realities. The manner in which these foundations are taught and practiced differs within traditions (Salzberg, 2017). (To experience practicing the four foundations directly, which is highly recommended, try this guided meditation: https://www.youtube.com/watch?v=E7W9XK-b5nQ).

The First Foundation (Body)

During this meditative training, to develop concentrative powers and elicit a relaxation response, one narrows their focus to a specific focal point or stimuli, commonly the breath. Even within the breath, the focal point can be further narrowed to the point where the breath enters and leaves the nostrils or the rising and falling of the abdomen. The purpose of the first foundation is to develop a sense of focused calm, which serves as a platform for the other foundations.

The Second Foundation (Sensations)

As one's concentration develops, the meditator then expands the scope of experience or telephoto lens of awareness, paying attention to the physical sensations that arise in the body, "specifically noting if the experience is pleasant, unpleasant, or neutral . . . one learns to override habitual reactive tendencies of clinging to the pleasant, avoiding the unpleasant, and becoming disinterested in the neutral" (Neale, 2017, p. 21). The idea of this foundation is to enhance equanimity or staying present without impulsive reactions.

The Third Foundation (Mind)

During this practice, one focuses awareness on the nature of mind itself, noticing and observing mental states as they arise (e.g., agitation, overstimulation, focused, afflicted). As Neale explains, "One learns to observe the states and qualities of awareness without being compelled by them, or needing to suppress them on the other" (p. 21). In much the same way one practices to override habitual reactions to physical sensations (clinging, avoiding), the third foundation trains an individual to avoid compulsive reactions to what is known as mental hindrances: restlessness, lethargy, greed, hostility, and doubt. This frees the awareness to investigate deeper insights and reveals what is known as the "so-called nature of the mind itself," which is described as "naturally clear and cognizant" (p. 21).

The Fourth Foundation (Realities)

During this final foundation, one memorizes and internalizes a list of psychological phenomena, elements, or realities and observes these realities as they surface during mediation. To help guide one through this process, consider the analogy of consciousness being like a movie screen, asking the meditator to objectively observe the contents that appear on this screen—arising and dissipation of thoughts, contemplating the power of choice provide by being mindful, self-mastery by noticing the openness or space in the mind, which enables breaking the patterns of habitual reaction.

Mindfulness Movement in the West

Buddhism became of interest to Westerners, including European philosophers, as early as the eighteenth century. By the 1950s, meditation teachers such as Maharishi Mahesh Yogi, who popularized Transcendental Meditation, began teaching their methods in the United States. Other teachers, such as Buddhist monk Chögyam Trungpa Rinpoche, who founded Naropa University in Colorado in 1972, also helped spread ideas of meditation and mindfulness to the West. However, Jon Kabat-Zinn, a molecular biologist who founded the Center for Mindfulness at the University of Massachusetts Medical School in 1979 and established the mindfulness-based stress reduction (MBSR) program to help patients suffering from chronic pain, is often largely credited with mainstreaming mindfulness in the United States. During the last several decades, there has been an increased interest in scientifically studying mindfulness in various secular settings, with advances in neuroscience assisting in what can be studied. To give a sense of this explosion in interest, the number of mindfulness articles appearing in academic journals grew from a single article in 1966 to 2,808 articles in 2020, with the majority of research occurring in the United States (Pratt, 2021). Much of the early research focused on how mindfulness worked as a practice or therapy, but has since shifted to examining factors that might make the practice more or less effective.

SCIENTIFIC BENEFITS OF MINDFULNESS

The practice of mindfulness has been shown to lower stress levels, boost immunity, reduce chronic pain, enhance emotional regulation, improve relationships, boost positive emotions and attitude, and improve concentration, attention, and memory (Baer et al., 2006; Creswell et al., 2007; Larrivee, 2012; Smalley & Winston, 2010). While mindfulness research is still considered in the early stages within the neuroscientific community, findings have been extremely promising (see table 1.2).

For instance, mindfulness meditation practices have produced structural changes in areas of the brain connected to learning and memory, impacting the density and volume of gray matter associated with various brain-related tasks (Hölzel et al., 2008; Lazar et al., 2005; Pagnoni & Cekic, 2007; Vestergaard-Poulsen et al., 2009). Lazar and colleagues (2005) found that after eight weeks of practice during a Mindfulness-Based Stress Reduction course participants experienced thickening in the posterior cingulate, the area of the brain associated with wandering and self-relevance; the hippocampus, which is responsible for learning, memory, cognition, and emotional regulation; and the temporoparietal junction, which is connected to empathy and compassion. Mindfulness meditation may also downgrade the amygdala, which houses the fear response mechanism in the brain and influences the body's fear, stress, and anxiety functions (Lagopolous et al., 2009).

A more recent study found that engaging in the MBSR program also worked to treat anxiety as taking a generic form of Lexapro, a drug commonly prescribed for depression and anxiety (Hoge et al., 2020). Both groups experienced about a 30 percent reduction in anxiety rates.

What Happens to the Brain When Engaging in Mindfulness Meditation?

The terms "mindfulness" and "meditation" are often used interchangeably, but mindfulness might be thought of as a quality that doesn't necessarily require sitting down in meditation—for example, *I am being mindful of my words. I am being mindful of my actions at work.* On the other hand, the term

Table 1.2. Summary of the Benefits of Mindfulness Meditation

Psychological	Physical
Improved memory	Reduced chronic pain
Reduced stress, reduced anxiety	Enhanced energy levels
Improved self-esteem	Improved immune system
Enhanced concentration and focus	Enhanced sleep
Improved mood/happiness	Improved digestion

"meditation" is often referred to as a formal practice or a method. Some meditation methods involve the direct use of mindfulness, for example, breath meditation or a body scan. Hall (2013) provides a succinct description of what goes on in our brains when engaging in mindfulness meditation:

- When closing our eyes, for example, and allowing our minds to settle down by focusing on the breath, activity increases in the attention association area of the brain, while activity decreases in the prefrontal cortex surrounding that area. Information deemed less important is filtered out, resulting in a state of focused attention and experience of present-centered or "present-now" awareness.
- We experience a shift in the brain from left-brain thinking (intellectualized) to right-brain functioning, as right-brain activity is primarily associated with attention.
- Decreased activity in the right parietal lobe, creating a "dissolution" of the self/non-self boundary. We also experience a loss of sense of time/space. This chain of events impacts the brain's limbic system, or emotional center. Since there's extensive connection between the parietal lobe orientation association area and the hippocampus, this in turn stimulates the amygdala, the brain's alarm system, assigns emotional significance to our experiences and controls activation of our fight-flight-or-freeze response. With no threat detected from the senses, the amygdala works through the brain's hypothalamus to modify the body's autonomic nervous system, resulting in the activation of the parasympathetic nervous system (the relaxation response). We experience a clear, alert state of mind, or a "blissful, peaceful state" (p. 30) as psychological effects, such as changes to the heart rate, breathing rate, and blood pressure, occur.

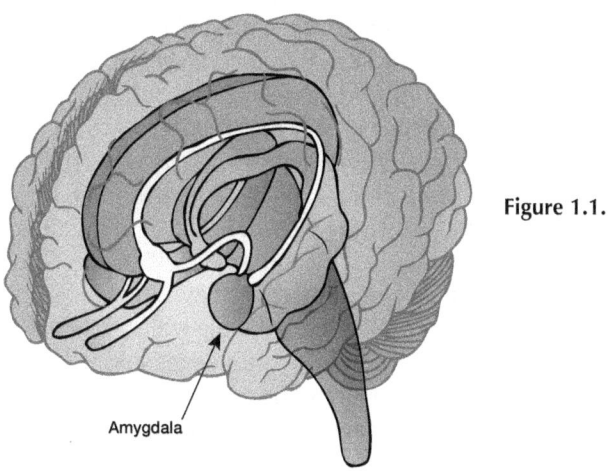

Figure 1.1.

MINDFULNESS'S RELEVANCE TO EDUCATIONAL SUPERVISION

During the last decade, there has been a rapid rise in the number of public schools implementing mindfulness-based programs or mindfulness-related curricula across the nation. Studies suggest mindfulness programs can enhance school-related skills, including executive function, working memory, sustained attention, and self-regulation (Albrecht et al., 2012; Bellinger et al., 2015; Schonert-Reich & Lawlor, 2010; Semple et al., 2017).

Teacher educators have also begun to use and study mindfulness approaches with teacher candidates and classroom teachers (Alderfer, 2015; Dorman et al., 2017; Korthagen et al., 2013), finding that participants generally experienced less stress, higher states of calm, and were more present for their students. Mindfulness can provide those entering the teaching profession with specific coping strategies helped them manage stress levels and improve self-esteem and feelings of competence (Villate & Butand, 2017). In addition, mindfulness can assist supervisors working in clinically based teacher-preparation settings by being more present during teaching observations and more attuned to the affective needs of teacher candidates (Haberlin, 2019). Mindfulness also can assist school leaders such as principals cope with the constant pressures of the role (Wells, 2013). Like Murphy (2017) learned when working with pre-service teachers, mindfulness would serve as a "unique entry point" for supervisors by "introducing and integrating contemplative practices to support well-being and success of individuals" (n.p.).

Despite movements within education circles to embrace mindfulness as a beneficial tool, it has not really permeated the field of instructional supervision (thus, the need for a book like this). For example, a search in the *Journal of Educational Supervision* archives produces no mention of the terms "mindfulness," "meditation," "consciousness," or "contemplative" in article titles. Popular supervision books, including *SuperVision and Instructional Leadership: A Developmental Approach*, 10th edition (Glickman et al., 2017); *Supervision: A Redefinition*, 8th edition (Sergiovanni & Starratt, 2007); *Effective Supervision: Supporting the Art & Science of Teaching* (Marzano et al., 2011); and *Supervision That Improves Teaching and Learning: Strategies and Techniques* (Sullivan & Glanz, 2005), are also largely absent the topic of mindfulness.

But exploring mindfulness-based approaches within the field of supervision makes sense. Intentional, present-centered awareness is a common dominator and an absolute necessity when working with teachers and preparing them for the classroom. When analyzing prominent supervision frameworks, it becomes apparent that someone serving a supervisory role (e.g., principal, university faculty, mentor teacher) must possess finely tuned awareness to perform a variety of functions, practices, and tasks. Present-centered awareness can complement a supervisor's need to be cognizant of a supervisee's developmental stage (Glickman et al., 2017); the social-emotional needs of supervisees and of when to employ the proper practice or task (Burns et al., 2019); and awareness of the moral implications or social justice issues within supervision (Glickman et al., 2017; Sergiovanni & Starratt, 2007). Effective supervisors must also be highly aware of their physical environment, the needs of the partnership school, the dynamic of a teacher's classroom, etc. (Sergiovanni & Starratt, 2007). In addition, mindfulness training could help a supervisor with self-awareness or "an internal awareness of one's cognitions and emotions" (Richards et al., 2010, p. 251).

Mindfulness's relevance to supervision becomes even more relevant when you consider the notion of recognition and choice. The skill to create a gap between what happens in supervision—perhaps a teacher struggles during an observed lesson, a principal lacks cultural responsiveness, a teacher candidate breaks down emotionally during a post-conference—can be of incredible value. Learning to step back and become aware of one's breath, of one's bodily responses (the onset of fight-flight-or-freeze), of one's emotions and thought patterns, can be a game-changer for a supervisor, empowering her to become conscious of deeply rooted patterns and unconscious, negative reactivity, and creating a space for fresh, more-supportive, enriching responses. In addition, learning to incorporate what are known as attitudes toward mindfulness, such as *beginner's mind*, *patience*, *non-judgment*, and *trust*, can transform the entire supervision landscape for an individual by creating new perspectives, more-presented centered perspectives and actions, and more-compassionate interactions (these mindfulness attitudes form the basis and structure of this book and will be explored in greater detail in subsequent chapters).

MINDFULNESS MOMENT

Periodically throughout the book, you will be asked to pause for a *mindfulness moment* and practice brief mindfulness-based techniques. It's one thing to read about mindfulness, but this quality requires firsthand experience to grasp. Therefore, readers are encouraged to pause and engage in the practice before continuing.

Simple Breath Awareness

Vipassana, sometimes called breath meditation or mindfulness meditation, is a technique of observing the breath. The method, originating from the Buddhist tradition, is described as a practical, secular technique that can produce feelings of calm and peace of mind (Vipassana Research Institute, n.d.). This mindfulness-based technique will be described in greater detail in chapter 3; but for now, try this introduction to using the breath to enhance the quality of mindfulness.

Begin by sitting in a comfortable position (it's not necessary to sit cross-legged on the floor; sitting in a chair will do). Keep your back straight but not stiff. Cup your hands or let them rest easily on the lap. Close your eyes or cast them downward. Gently bring your awareness to the manner in which the breath naturally enters and exists the nostrils. Don't try to control the breath or change it; just witness or observe the natural flow already happening. If you become distracted or caught up in thoughts, bring your attention back to the rhythm of the breath. After a few minutes, allow your awareness to come off the breath; stretch the body, getting up when ready.

THE STRUCTURE OF THIS BOOK: NINE ATTITUDES OF MINDFULNESS

Nine attitudinal factors "constitute the major pillars of mindful practice" (Kabat-Zinn, 2005, p. 31): non-judging, gratitude, patience, beginner's mind, trust, acceptance, non-striving, letting go, and generosity. The attitudes are consciously cultivated as one practices mindfulness-based methods. These mindfulness attitudes are not independent of one another; rather, each one influences and relies on the others. The nine attitudes can also serve as an effective framework to support how mindfulness can be infused and woven into the fabric of various supervisory practices and, hence, provide the structure for this book. Each chapter is designed upon one or more of these attitudes, with the exception of chapter 2, which explores how the concept of presence within supervision can be enhanced through mindfulness practices.

WHAT TO EXPECT IN THIS BOOK

Chapter 2: A Brief Overview of Instructional Supervision (and Where Mindfulness Fits In)

To understand the usefulness and possibilities of mindfulness in the coaching of educational leaders and teachers, an overview of supervision, including its prominent models and views, along with its present challenges, is needed. In this chapter, a brief overview of educational supervision is provided, with a snapshot of how supervision practices and paradigms have evolved and the current state of supervision. The chapter concludes with how mindfulness-based practices can enhance supervision and assist with the field's current challenges.

Chapter 3: Developing a Personal Mindfulness Practice

In this foundational chapter, you will learn how to skillfully design and implement your own personalized mindfulness meditation practice. While each chapter provides different mindfulness-based practices, strategies, and activities to cultivate the mindfulness attitudes, all of these approaches rest on the pillar of one's own daily practice. This chapter will answer all the basic questions about mindfulness meditation, such as what method is best, when and where to practice, how long to practice, and how to know whether your approach is working.

Chapter 4: Presence in Supervision

Presence is that unseen, magical element in supervision. Defined as the "way in which we occupy space, as well as the way we flow and move" (Helminski, 2000, pp. ix–xi), presence involves openness to possibility, availability, warmth, and deep listening—qualities essential to effectively coaching those in education to work with pre-K to grade 12 students. This chapter explores presence within the context of preparing teachers and how mindfulness practices cultivate these presence-related qualities.

Chapter 5: Beginner's Mind in Supervision

The first of the nine mindfulness attitudes, beginner's mind asks us to approach each situation and moment with openness, curiosity, and freshness. This state of mind enables an individual to operate more in the present moment with flexibility and creative responsiveness. During this chapter, readers consider how a beginner's mind—assisted by mindfulness-based practices—can enhance the supervision process.

Chapter 6: Patience and Trust in Supervision

Patience, or understanding and accepting that "sometimes things must unfold in their own time" (Kabat-Zinn, 2013, p. 23), is necessary whether coaching a teacher candidate to be ready to assume their own classroom or guiding an experienced teacher to hone their skills. Trust means listening to one's own feelings and intuition, which, in the context of supervision, means listening and collaborating with others but ultimately relying on one's inner guide in making decisions in the field. Mindfulness practices can help us cultivate patience and trust.

Chapter 7: Letting Go and Non-Striving as a Supervisor

Non-striving is not being attached to a specific outcome or purpose and using one's attention and energy wisely. This may seem contradictory to the role of supervision, which is generally defined as assisting teachers in instruction and leading to improve student outcomes. However, this attitude of non-striving allows us to explore the paradox of doing less and accomplishing more, of backing off from being so narrowly focused on outcomes and allowing goals to happen more in their own time. Similarly, the attitude of letting go, or nonattachment, means moving in a direction within supervision but also being open to new avenues and possibilities and not forcing our own beliefs, views, and potential bias on the situation.

Chapter 8: Acceptance and Non-Judgment

The notion of acceptance means the willingness to "see things as they are" in the present moment. From there, one is able to act appropriately, to know how to respond realistically to what is happening. Acceptance in the context of mindfulness does not mean passively accepting situations without changing them or acting. In supervision, this can mean seeing situations honestly and accurately—whether that's a teacher who is struggling in a classroom or a principal unwilling to act in a culturally responsive manner—and then acting from that space. Non-judgment requires you to become aware of the constant stream of judging and reacting to inner and outer experiences that we are all normally caught up in and to learn to step back from it. When we begin paying attention to the activity of our own mind, it is common to discover and be surprised by the fact that we are constantly generating judgments about our experience. As a supervisor, cultivating the skill to be an impartial witness to practice, at least at times, can serve as a tremendous advantage.

Chapter 9: Gratitude and Generosity (Yes, in Supervision)

Practicing gratitude has been shown to provide us with more energy and allow us to experience higher levels of well-being and less stress. Mindfulness-based gratitude involves noticing the small things and appreciating them in each moment. This attitude can provide supervisors with the energy and resilience needed to perform this challenging role. Generosity within the framework of mindfulness means consciously giving on various levels, including giving to oneself in the form of self-care and giving support, compassion, and attention to those supervised.

Chapter 10: Mindfulness-Informed Educational Leadership: Moving Toward a More Inclusive Approach to Supervision

In this final chapter you will receive a brief recap of the mindfulness attitudes and how they can inform supervision. The conversation will move toward how mindfulness practices can support encouraging a more-inclusive approach to preparing teachers and teaching students by sharing contemplative tools to inspire more awareness-based leadership. Various mindfulness meditation practices focusing on increasing compassion, inclusion, and equity are provided.

Chapter Two

A Brief History of Supervision and Overview of Supervision Models

(and Where Mindfulness-Based Supervision Fits In)

DEFINING SUPERVISION

The term "supervision" originates from two Latin words: *super* ("over") and *videre* ("to view"). Whether supervision is a role, a position, or a series of tasks or functions has been debated. The author subscribes to Sergiovanni and Starratt's assertion that supervision "is best understood as both a role and a function" (2007, p. 5). For example, a school principal enacts a formal supervisory role when engaging in observations, conducting formal evaluations, and demonstrating instructional strategies. However, others not in formal supervisory roles can also engage in supervisory functions; for instance, a teacher engages in supervision when visiting a colleague's classroom to suggest teaching techniques or analyzing a lesson plan (p. 5). There's also no agreed-upon definition of supervision, though it's generally described as the endgame being to improve teaching and student achievement. Following are some ways in which supervision has been described in professional literature.

- "An organizational function concerned with promoting teacher growth, leading to improvement in teaching performance and greater student learning. Supervision is not concerned with making global judgments concerning the teacher's competence and performance" (Nolan & Hoover, 2011, p. 6).
- "Assistance for the enhancement of teaching and learning" (Glickman, Gordon & Ross-Gordon, 2013, p. 9).
- "Assistance or hand of help given to a professional colleague, the teacher in the process of teaching" (Runcan, 2013, pp. 4–6).

Those serving in supervisory roles perform a variety of functions, including facilitating pre- and post-conferences, professional development activities (e.g., leading seminars and workshops), gathering data as part of research, and portfolio development (Mette et al., 2017). Supervision is complex, featuring many inherent challenges, including navigating the transition from classroom teacher to a supervisor of teachers (Bullock, 2012; Williams, Ritter & Bullock, 2007, 2009). Additionally, supervisors often tread the line between carrying out evaluation duties and serving as a supportive guide or coach.

A HISTORICAL SNAPSHOT OF SUPERVISION

The practice of instructional supervision can be traced to at least the 1700s, where the term "inspector" appeared in writings about education (Grumet, 1979). Supervision during this period involved "strict control and close inspection of school facilities" (Sullivan, 2004, p. 7). Often, one teacher at school took on administrative duties, and this role morphed into a school principal position (Marzano, Frontier & Livingston, 2011). During the 1800s, schools relied on clergy to supervise schools, believing they possessed the necessary education and experience from leading religious schools. However, this practice came under question, as clergy were no longer believed to have the subject area knowledge or expertise required to judge teacher effectiveness (Marzano, Frontier & Livingston, 2011). As the American education system massively expanded during the Industrial Revolution, supervisory responsibilities fell to school superintendents (Sullivan, 2004). As a result, schools became centralized bureaucracies, with superintendents justifying their existence through supervision (Glanz, 1991).

By the early twentieth century, education and instructional supervision became heavily influenced by Fredrick Taylor's scientific views of management. "Led by Edward Thorndike, educators began to view measurement as the ultimate tool for a more scientific approach to schooling" (Marzano, Frontier & Livingston, 2011, p. 14). While a proper treatment of the historical perspectives of supervision in schools could fill volumes, the purpose of this chapter is to provide a brief overview of the field. In order to see where the field is headed, and how mindfulness-based supervision fits into the greater landscape, we must first consider where supervision has been. It's pertinent to know that supervision has gone "through a number of developmental periods during the past 300 years" (Burnham, 2001, p. 301). To organize this historical perspective in a succinct, reader-friendly manner, the next section draws upon Burnham's work, which skillfully organizes supervision practices into epochs. In addition, to help readers conceptualize the theoretical changes in supervision paradigms, frameworks, and models, Glanz's (2000) work is also utilized. Table 2.1 provides a snapshot of the historical perspectives of supervision.

Table 2.1. Pivotal Periods of Instructional Supervision

Period	Delineating Characteristics
Period of School Supervision (or Administrative Inspection)	• Supervision is conducted by religious officers/clergy/laypersons from the community. • Focus is on controlling standards. • Concerned with management of schools. • Helping teacher practice/teacher growth is not emphasized.
Period of Efficiency in Supervision	• Responsibility of supervision shifts from layperson to school personnel (e.g., principal or head teachers were assigned to visit classrooms and supervise). • As new subjects are introduced to curriculum, focus is placed on improving instruction. • Classroom visitations, observations, and demonstrations become common practice. • Supervision as inspection or transfer of superior knowledge remains the dominant paradigm.
Period of Cooperation/Collaboration	• Expansion of the curriculum (fine arts, physical education, foreign languages) results in creation of a special supervisor position. • Increased responsibilities make cooperation and collaboration essential. • Assistant superintendents, principals, curriculum coordinators, and others work together to conduct supervisory tasks. • Supervision is now conceptualized as a democratic, cooperative, and creative process.
Period of Research-Based Supervision	• Technological advancements, federal grants, and competing space research among countries fuel extensive study of supervision. • Research is geared toward role perceptions of those in supervisory roles. • Questions are raised about the role and function of supervisors, and confusion remains about the role. • Behavioral science theory and research is used within supervision practices and frameworks.
Later Developments in Supervision	• General consensus that supervision is not the sole responsibility of one individual but rather a collective endeavor. • Developmental supervision—or gearing supervisory practices toward the individual and current stage of development—becomes a prominent concept. • Clinical supervision becomes a major model or approach. • The focus of supervision still remains on the improvement of instruction and student learning.

EVOLVING VIEWS OF SUPERVISION

In addition to considering the historical periods of supervision, it might also help to study the evolution of supervision from a purely conceptual or paradigm viewpoint. To provide this snapshot, Glanz (2000) has sorted supervision into three eras: premodern, modern, and postmodern (see table 2.2).

Premodern Era

During the premodern era, supervision was synonymous with inspection (Glanz, 2000). Bureaucratic supervision, or relying on inspectional methods, "dominated" discourse in the field until about 1920 (Sullivan, 2004, p. 15), and rather than improvement of instruction, the focus during the premodern era was removing inefficient teachers (Glanz, 2000). During this time, supervision was situated within an imbalanced power differential and a clear hierarchy between supervisor and supervisee.

Modern Era

Conceptually, the modern era represents a movement toward better democratizing supervision while minimizing evaluative functions. "Supervisors tried to change their image as 'snoopervisors' by adopting alternate methods of supervision" (Glanz, 2000, p. 73). Supervisory practices were largely influenced by John Dewey (1929) and other intellectuals of the time, who espoused democratic, scientific thinking, and James Hosic (1920), who encouraged democratic supervision. This new paradigm took form in a number of ways, including Glickman's (1981) developmental model, which was based on the notion that supervisors needed to "be more mindful of the developmental stages of teachers" (p. 6). Other models emerging from this paradigm included *cognitive coaching*, a "nonjudgmental, developmental, reflective model" (Costa & Garmston, 1989, p. 5) grounded in humanistic and cognitive theories. Cognitive coaching features supervisors and teachers engaging in a cycle of planning and reflecting conversations.

Postmodern Era

The postmodern era features a paradigm where supervision is viewed as overly technical in nature (Glanz, 2000). Instead, the postmodern view might embrace dialogic supervision (Waite, 1995), where the supervisor focuses more on the relationship with the teacher candidate rather than data and serving more as a witness to teaching for the purpose of engaging in

Table 2.2. Evolving Eras of Supervision

Era	Characteristics	Examples of Associated Views/Models/Paradigms
Premodern	Bureaucratic, controlling, supervision through inspection, lack of autonomy, evaluative.	*Behavioristic teacher education* (Zeichner, 1983)
Modern	Dissatisfied with premodern approach; emphasis on growth of the teacher, collegiality, relationship-focused, autonomy.	*Developmental supervision* Glickman (1981); *Cognitive coaching* (Costa & Garmston, 1989)
Postmodern	Modern views seen as overly technical; emphasis on relationship, particular language used.	Moving away from the term "supervision" (Glickman, 1992; Gordon, 1997); *Dialogic supervision* (Waite, 1995)

that dialogue. Postmodern scholars have even suggested eliminating the term "supervision," instead favoring the phrase "instructional leadership" (Glickman, 1992; Gordon, 1997).

THE CURRENT STATE OF SUPERVISION

In recent years, the field of supervision has faced various challenges. Radical changes and disruptions, including the COVID-19 pandemic, which forced public schools across the nation to suddenly transition to online-learning platforms, has caused the field of supervision to reflect and reconsider the preparation of principals and teachers, particularly how BIPOC (Black, indigenous, and people of color) students have been serviced in recent decades (Mette, 2020). There has been an increased interest and push for culturally responsive supervision and equity-minded supervision. As Livers and colleagues (2022) wrote:

> As it relates to clinical experiences in teacher education, we have learned that we must recreate supervision, a key component, to address the lived realities and inherent potential of historically marginalized and exploited children, families, and communities. To reach the full potential of equity minded supervision, there must be a shift from culturally blind supervisory practices toward explicit scaffolding of culturally responsive enactments as part of a freedom-minded framework of clinical supervision in teacher education. (p. 4)

As of the writing of this book, educational supervision's future remains unclear and the field continues to face additional challenges.

Supervision continues to struggle with identifying its proper name and establishing its niche within the larger framework of education (Glanz, 2021). For instance, questions arise whether supervision should be combined with the term "instructional leadership" or promoted as its own entity.

On a related note, senior scholars of supervision disagree on whether supervision needs to operate as a unique field or continue, as Hazi put it, "to travel incognito, being overshadowed by school administration" (Glanz, 2018, p. 10). Scholars seem cautiously optimistic about the field's future, citing a lack of research and empirical evidence. Supervision scholars continue to try increase membership in the Council of Professors of Supervision (COPIS), the single association in the field, and promote its academic journal, *The Journal of Educational Supervision* (Gordon, 2019).

HOW CAN MINDFULNESS HELP THE FIELD OF SUPERVISION?

Mindfulness is certainly not a silver bullet, and this is the case when it comes to the challenges of supervision. What mindfulness-based practices can do is offer tools to enhance awareness and help school leaders operate more from the present moment, with more compassion and connectedness. The strength of mindfulness practice within the context of supervision exists within the individual—for example, the principal charged with developing, managing, and empowering teachers and creating a culturally responsive campus. Mindfulness practices that encourage one to authentically face their own inherent biases and prejudices (Magee, 2019; Owens, 2020) could be utilized by school leaders to engage in *critical self-reflection* (Khalifa, 2020) needed to cultivate the *critical consciousness* for positive change to occur on campuses (Brown, 2004; Dantley, 2005a; Gay & Kirkland, 2003; McKenzie et al., 2008). While this topic will be elaborated in chapter 10, the main focus of this book is how mindfulness can be practiced with the commonly used Clinical Model of supervision used to prepare teachers (those who currently work in classrooms) and teacher candidates (those enrolled in university and college preparation programs).

THE CLINICAL SUPERVISION MODEL

There are a number of prominent supervision models, including Sergiovanni and Starratt's Supervisory Leadership Framework, Marzano's Teacher Expertise Model, the Glickman and Gordon and Gordon's Developmental Supervision Model, and the Scope and the Nature of Teacher Candidate Supervision Framework (Burns, Jacobs & Yendol-Hoppey, 2019). All of these models have their merit and possibly could be enhanced by infusing mindfulness-based practices. However, additional description is provided here for the Clinical Model of Supervision, the oldest and best known model, as it seems a fitting starting point and practical framework for how supervisors might practically bring mindfulness into the preparation of educators. Borrowing the term "clinical" from the medical profession, Cogan and Goldhammer from Harvard University began using a clinical approach to preparing teachers in the 1960s (Pajak, 2000). Clinical supervision has been increasingly used by university-based supervisors, principals, mentor teachers, and peer teachers. Variations exist around the implementation of the model; however, the five-step sequence or steps proposed by Goldhammer (1969) remains most widely practiced. Clinical supervision has been described as a "form of coaching" (Sergiovanni & Starratt, 2007, p. 232), as it is highly collaborative in nature and can conducted by a school principal, a university-based supervisor, a fellow teacher, or, as is often the case, a combination of these individuals working together. While taking various forms, clinical supervision is classroom-based, grounded in face-to-face relationships with teachers, and aimed at improving teacher effectiveness and enhancing professional growth (Goldhammer, 1969; Sergiovanni & Starratt, 2007). Supervisors using this model might use both summative and formative evaluations to gather and provide feedback to teachers and teacher candidates. As described briefly in table 2.3, at the heart of clinical supervision is the five-stage cycle: (1) pre-observation conference, (2) classroom observation, (3) analysis of that observation, (4) post-observation conference, and (5) post-conference analysis (Sergiovanni & Starratt, 2007, p. 238). However, due to time constraints, supervisors may engage in an abridged version of this cycle or complete only certain steps.

Pre-Observation Conference (Stage 1)

During this stage, the teacher or teacher candidate describes the upcoming lesson that will be observed, including the student learning objectives and how those objectives will be assessed or measured, the content, and the teaching strategies used. The supervisor's role during this stage is to ask clarifying and probing questions to better understand the teacher's instructional plan and goals for the lesson. The supervisor should also consider what type of data will be collected during the classroom observation (e.g., teacher/student behaviors, student work samples, movement patterns) and the data-collection tools needed (e.g., checklists, anecdotal notes, videotaping) (Pajak, 2000).

Classroom Observation (Stage 2)

The supervisor observes the teacher or teacher candidate in action, teaching the lesson that was discussed during the pre-conference. According to Pajak (2000), during this stage the teacher's task is to teach the lesson as well as possible, while the supervisor should record the teaching events accurately as possible.

Data Analysis and Strategy (Stage 3)

At this point in the cycle, the teacher is encouraged to reflect on the lesson and analyze data that demonstrates that student learning outcomes were achieved (e.g., student work samples, test scores). The supervisor analyzes the data collected during the lesson using observation rubrics, checklist, or other tools.

Conference (Stage 4)

During this stage, the supervisor and teacher discuss the observed lesson. Pajak (2000) suggests that the teacher keep an open mind regarding the behaviors and events occurring during the observation. The supervisor attempts to clarify and build upon this understanding. One aspect of the lesson likely to be addressed during the conference would be whether student learning outcomes were achieved and what contributed toward that end or what prevented that from happening.

Post-Analysis (Stage 5)

During the final stage, the teacher's task is to honestly share their evaluation of the clinical cycle and how it went. Using this feedback and their own reflective powers, the supervisor should critically examine their own performance during this cycle.

THE CONVERGENCE OF MINDFULNESS AND THE CLINICAL SUPERVISION CYCLE

The five stages of the clinical cycle, particularly the pre-conference, observation, and post-conference, will be used in each chapter to frame how

Table 2.3. Five Stages of Clinical Supervision Model

Clinical Model Stage	Teacher Task	Supervisor Task
Pre-Conference	Mentally rehearse and orally describe the upcoming lesson, including purpose and content.	Understand what the teacher has in mind for the planned lesson through asking probing and clarifying questions.
Classroom Observation	Teach the lesson as well as possible.	Collect data on the lesson as accurately as possible.
Data Analysis/Strategy	Make sense of the data.	Make sense of the data/plan for the post-conference.
Post-Conference	Critically examine the observed lesson, reflect, and plan for the next lesson.	Clarify and build on the teacher's understanding of what occurred during the lesson, what led to student learning.
Post-Conference Analysis	Provide honest feedback to the supervisor about how the clinical cycle went.	Critically examine their own performance during the clinical cycle.

Note: Adapted from Pajak, 2003

mindfulness attitudes and mindfulness-based practices can inform the supervisory process. The Four Foundations of Mindfulness, for example, provide a framework for mindsets, approaches, and tools that can inform each stage of supervision. For example, the first foundation, mindfulness of breathing, applied to stage two of the clinical process, could mean using the breath as an anchor, allowing it to settle down on the present-moment experience (the classroom lesson unfolding). The supervisor could bring the distracted mind back to the teaching, thus strengthening their observational skills and perceptive abilities. Similarly, the second foundation, mindfulness of sensation, could be applied to different stages. The supervisor would be discreetly aware of their subtle sensations and feelings that arise as they interact with the teacher or teacher candidate. Perhaps an unpleasant feeling emerges, signaling that the supervisor is not comfortable with an aspect of the instructional plan presented, or a neutral feeling about the teaching methods used. However, rather than engage in habitual emotional reactivity (likely further complicating or aggravating the situation), the supervisor can respond in a more open, caring, and supportive manner. Table 2.4 illustrates specific examples of how each of the four foundations of mindfulness can inform the stages of the clinical cycle.

Table 2.4. Foundations of Mindfulness Supporting the Clinical Supervision Cycle

Clinical Cycle Stage	Foundations of Mindfulness Applications
Pre-Observation Conference (*Stage 1*)	*Mindfulness of Body* • Supervisor utilizes breath and body to remain focused, grounded, and present during conference, eliciting a "sense of relaxation" and "fundamental safety" (Neale, 2018, p. 20). *Mindfulness of Feeling* • Supervisor becomes aware of the sensations, feelings, and emotions that arise during interaction with the teacher, learning to "override habitual reactive tendencies" (Neale, 2018, p. 20). *Mindfulness of Mind* • Supervisor practices awareness of mental states as they emerge, noticing these states and qualities of awareness without being compelled by them or needing to suppress them. Like the second foundation using the body, "one learns to decondition automatic reactions" (Neale, 2018, p. 21). *Mindfulness of Phenomena* • While undoubtedly more complex, the supervisor could reflect upon and memorize different psychological realities and supervision best practices and principles and watch for them to arise. For instance, they might observe how providing specific, purposeful feedback emerges during the conference and how that impacts the teacher and the overall outcome.
Classroom Observation (*Stage 2*)	*Mindfulness of Body (Breathing):* • Supervisor utilizes breath and body to remain focused, grounded, and present during the classroom observation, eliciting a "sense of relaxation" and "fundamental safety" (Neale, 2018, p. 20). *Mindfulness of Feeling* • Supervisor becomes aware of the sensations, feelings, and emotions that arise during the observation, taking note and reflecting on these reactions before meeting with the teacher. *Mindfulness of Mind* • Supervisor practices awareness of mental states as they emerge during the observation, noticing when these states and qualities of awareness arise and in within what context, providing a deeper, intuitive layer of observational data. *Mindfulness of Phenomena* • Supervisor could reflect upon and memorize realities connected to teaching best practices and watch for them to emerge during the observation.
Data Analysis and Strategy (*Stage 3*)	*Mindfulness of Body* • Supervisor utilizes breath and body to intensely concentrate and analyze the data collected during the observation.

Clinical Cycle Stage	Foundations of Mindfulness Applications
	Mindfulness of Feeling • Supervisor is consciously aware of the sensations that arise when analyzing the data, taking note of what might produce pleasant, unpleasant, and neutral feelings. *Mindfulness of Mind* • Supervisor is mindful of states of mind that emerge during the data analysis process. *Mindfulness of Phenomena* • The supervisor keeps in mind best practices and core themes of instructional supervision and teaching as they analyze the data.
Conference (*Stage 4*)	*Mindfulness of Body* • Like during the pre-conference, the supervisor utilizes breath and body to remain focused, grounded, and present during the conference, eliciting a "sense of relaxation" and "fundamental safety" (Neale, 2018, p. 20). *Mindfulness of Feeling* • Similarly, the supervisor is aware of the sensations, feelings, and emotions that arise during the conference with the teacher, learning to "override habitual reactive tendencies" (Neale, 2018, p. 20). *Mindfulness of Mind* • Supervisor is also aware of mental states as they emerge during the conference, noticing these states and qualities of awareness without being compelled by them or needing to suppress them. Thus, the supervisor is mindful of the feedback given and the language and tone used. • The supervisor is mindful of supervision and teaching themes and concepts reflected on during the pre-conference and implemented during the observation, watching for whether those constructs arise.
Post-Analysis (*Stage 5*)	*Mindfulness of Body* • Supervisor utilizes breath and body to center themselves and remain present with authentic feedback about the cycle process and keep focused on their own self-evaluation. *Mindfulness of Feeling* • Supervisor practices awareness of possible habitual reactions and negative emotional patterns felt or experienced when reflecting on the cycle process and their role, thus establishing a base for more positive, productive responses and actions. *Mindfulness of Mind* • Similarly, the supervisor monitors mental states when reflecting and receiving feedback on the cycle process, observing their reactions. *Mindfulness of Phenomena* • Finally, the supervisor observes whether potential supervision and teaching themes and fundamental concepts were present in the cycle process.

The Six Immediate Response Skills

In their research, Burns and Badiali (2016a, 2016b) discovered a set of leadership skills that "can improve instructional practice *during* the act of teaching" and enable leaders to "break down the complexity of teaching for others by capitalizing on teachable moments for teachers to improve their practice" (Glickman & Burns, 2020, p. 106). The Six Immediate Response Skills are noticing, ignoring, intervening, pointing, unpacking, and processing. Table 2.5 provides a brief description of each skill, an example, and how mindfulness might enhance that skill. Along with the stages of the Clinical Supervision Cycle, these response skills will also be referenced throughout the book to frame and contextualize various mindfulness attitudes and practices. Knowledge of these skills deepens our exploration of mindfulness supervision as they intensify a supervisor's ability to respond live, in the present moment, to what is unfolding in the classroom.

With a brief history of educational supervision and conception of how supervision models and approaches have evolved, along with using the Clinical Model stages and immediate response skills as a contextual framework, you can begin to see how mindfulness-based techniques can support one's leadership work with teachers. In the next chapter we will begin to examine how the mindfulness attitude further enhances supervision and learn specific methods to cultivate these attitudes.

A MINDFUL MOMENT

After learning about the Four Foundations of Mindfulness and seeing how they might support the five stages of the Clinical Supervision Model, try these brief mindfulness exercises to begin to experience the foundations and how they practice awareness of different aspects of the human experience (e.g., the body, feelings, mental states).

Sit in a comfortable position, either in a chair or on a meditation cushion on the floor. Close your eyes or cast them downward. Gently bring your awareness to the breath, following the in-and-out flow. Do this for several minutes. Shift your awareness to the body. Place your attention on the top of your head and mentally scan down through your eyes, nose, mouth, and to your jaw. Continue to scan down your body, becoming aware of any sensations, tension, feelings of ease. Go down the chest, the stomach, the torso, down through the legs. Let your attention settle in your feet. Bring your awareness back to the head, to your thoughts. Become mindful of how the thoughts come and go. Don't try to change them. Just observe them, imagining the

Table 2.5. Six Immediate Response Skills

Skill	Description	Example	Mindfulness Connection
Noticing	The ability to see important moments in teaching that can lead to teacher learning	Teacher is conferencing with student. Classroom is noisy, making it difficult to conference.	Encouraging a calm, open mind more conducive to noticing
Ignoring	The ability to intentionally decide not to act on something that is noticed (as to not overwhelm the teacher when giving feedback)	Teacher notices student learning stations are unorganized, students off task, but ignores these issues in order to discuss the large amount of homework assignments (in the turn-in bin) not being graded.	Increased awareness of judging and reactivity
Intervening	The ability to act in the moment to improve instruction and support student learning	A few students are constantly having side conversations, disrupting other students' learning. Novice teacher is trying to work with another group of students. You walk over to the off-task students to see if your proximity changes their behavior.	Cultivating the ability to be more in the present moment
Pointing	The ability to draw teacher's attention to a teachable moment	Whisper coaching (or bug-in-the-ear technology) is used to note when, for example, a teacher asked a high-quality question.	Ability to connect with others with compassion and intentionality
Unpacking	The ability to break down a teachable moment for the teacher	Help the teacher understand why a science lesson worked well and led to student learning outcomes.	Increasing the ability to listen deeply and be in tune with development of the teacher
Processing	The ability to lead a reflective conversation with the teacher to determine what happened in the lesson and next steps	Teacher is asked, "What would you do differently if you taught this lesson again?"	Ability to connect and listen deeply

mind as a movie screen and thoughts as passing images. Become aware of your mental state; for example, is the focus narrow or more open? Return your attention to the breath. Sit for a minute, just aware of the breath, the body, and mind. Open your eyes when ready.[1]

WHAT'S NEXT?

In chapter 3 you will study how to establish a personal mindfulness meditation practice as a foundation for mindfulness-based supervision.

---

1. For a more in-depth guided meditation for the Four Foundations of Mindfulness, check out this video by Miles Neale, a Buddhist psychotherapist and meditation teacher: https://www.youtube.com/watch?v=E7W9XK-b5nQ.

Chapter Three

Developing a Personal Mindfulness Meditation Practice

Before delving into the mindfulness attitudes, this chapter serves as a foundation, guiding you through how exactly to establish your own mindfulness meditation practice. While mindfulness can be practiced in daily life, it is highly recommended that you consider engaging in formal mindfulness meditation. Think of this step as building the legs of a table and a solid top, then the various mindfulness attitude practices and supervision strategies can be securely piled on this table. Without dedicating yourself to your own regular meditation practice, you might feel as though you have nowhere to place or arrange these ideas and strategies. Regularly engaging in a formalized mindfulness meditation practice will provide a sustained, deeper experience, which will provide a range of benefits and help you connect to the ideas in the remaining chapters.

Establishing a mindfulness meditation practice does involve experimentation; there is no one-size-fits-all approach, as individuals have different needs, goals, temperaments, and lifestyles. When first considering the "right" practice, one challenge is that there are many meditation methods, originating from different traditions. Finding what works for you requires firsthand experience. You must also consider such logistics as how often and how long to meditate, when and where to meditate, and how to gauge whether the practice is benefiting you. This chapter will help with those questions.

WHAT EXACTLY IS MEDITATION?

Meditation has been defined in many ways. The Sanskrit word for meditation, *dhyana*, has been translated as "meaning to train the mind." The Tibetan word for meditation, *gom*, means "to become familiar with" the mind. In the West, meditation has evolved into an umbrella term for practicing various methods to calm the mind and reduce stress. For the purposes of this book, consider meditation as a settled state of mind—essentially a state of non-doing, where there is no mental or physical activity. During meditation, "your mind settles to tranquility, and your body becomes still. Your body is more relaxed, often more deeply than sleep, yet your mind is more alert than wakefulness. Your awareness expands" (Shumsky, 2001, n.p.).

Meditation can be found in cultures and traditions around the world throughout history. It's believed that forms of meditation date back thousands of years, possibly "as old as humanity itself" based on the potential meditative capacities of Neanderthals (Meade, 2019, n.p.). While it is not the intent of this book to provide a comprehensive description of meditation traditions, table 3.1 presents a brief overview.

While the terms "meditation" and "mindfulness" are sometimes used interchangeably, they are not the same. Mindfulness is a quality or psychological trait of present-moment awareness. One can be mindful driving a car, during a conversation, or washing dishes. On the other hand, meditation is generally considered a formal method or practice and may—or may not—involve the use of mindfulness. For example, forms of meditation are *zazen*, where Zen Buddhists sit in particular postures for long periods of time using meditative techniques. Another method of meditation is Transcendental Meditation, where practitioners sit for 15 to 20 minutes, mentally reciting a sound, or *mantra*. This chapter will focus on formal mindfulness meditation methods; however, readers should be encouraged to explore various methods and techniques that are suitable.

Table 3.1. Brief Overview of Meditation Traditions

Tradition	Methods
Vedic	Dating back thousands of years, meditation can be found in the *Veda* produced in ancient India. Transcendental Meditation finds its roots in the Vedic tradition.
Hinduism	Meditation is practiced in various forms of yoga, including Hatha Yoga, in which practitioners lie on their backs after a session in meditation.
Buddhism	Meditation is most associated with Buddhism. Born 26 centuries ago, the Buddha is believed to have studied meditation techniques from different teachers and developed his own methods.
Islamic	Various meditation techniques, including *whirling*, practiced by a sect called Sufis, have originated from the Islamic tradition.
Christianity	References to "meditate" are found in the Bible. One practice, *Lectio Divina*, or "divine reading," involves reading verses of scripture and then reflecting and praying on them.
Taoism	Meditation methods that involve circulating *chi* (energy) and promoting balance and harmony are practiced with the ancient Chinese philosophy of Taoism.

CHOOSING A MINDFULNESS MEDITATION METHOD

Selecting a suitable meditation method can be challenging, since there are different methods available. Mindfulness-based meditation techniques include breath awareness (explained at the end of the chapter), loving-kindness meditation, and body awareness (also covered later in the book). However, mindfulness meditation practice can involve movement; for example, walking meditation, yoga, and the Chinese health systems of Tai Chi and Qigong. Finding a qualified teacher to guide you in learning a meditation method is advisable. However, if that is not possible, there are many resources to help you get started. An important consideration before beginning any meditation practice is determining *why* you might start meditating and what you hope to gain. The following Meditation Self-Assessment (Williams, 2018) asks you to consider such questions as:

What do you feel is lacking in your life?
How does your body feel? Are there any places where it feels heavy or stuck?
Do you have a lot on your mind, more than usual?
Do you need help focusing?
How do you want to feel? Nourished, connected, energized, purposeful, etc.?

Other considerations include how much time you can dedicate to meditation, given your current schedule and present energy level.

EXPERIMENTATION WITH MEDITATION METHODS

At some point after researching, the only way to truly determine what meditation method bests suits you is to try some. Meditation is a very personalized, subjective experience. Pick a method, try it for a week or so, and see how you feel. Did you resonate with the method? Do you gain some sense of relaxation or feel better after practicing? If a certain method "feels right," commit to it for several months. Allow it to become part of your daily routine. Several mindfulness-based meditation methods will be explained at the end of this chapter, along with guided instructions.

How Long Should You Meditate?

After finding a method that works for you, a common question is "How long should I meditate?" The answer can vary based on the method and tradition, as well as your current level of experience and temperament. Meditation teachers generally suggest starting with very short periods of time, perhaps

5 or 10 minutes, and gradually increasing the time. Ideally, spending 15 to 20 minutes in the morning in meditation can produce benefits. If possible, adding another similar meditation session to the evening, to relieve stress and clear the mind after the workday is finished, can be very helpful.

Where to Meditate?

Creating a designated space—a corner, a room, or outdoor area—can enhance your meditation practice. Meditating in the same place each day creates a supportive energy and informs the mind that it is time to settle and quiet. Bring inspiring photographs, statutes, and other objects to the space. Decorate it with flowers, bowls of fruit, and other living things. You can add a comfortable chair or meditation cushions or yoga mats. Remember, meditation can be done wherever you are, but establishing a dedicated space at home can support practice.

When to Meditate?

Often, the best time to meditate is in the morning, before the busyness of the day. This sets a calming, positive tone. Another ideal time to meditate is in the evening, prior to dinner. Nevertheless, meditation can be practiced whenever you find time. Also, a little is better than nothing. If you are pressed for time, try meditating for even a few minutes; as Hall (2013) notes, "a little mindfulness can go a long way" (p. 47). If you miss a morning or evening session, just pick it back up the next day.

HOW DO YOU KNOW YOUR MEDITATION IS WORKING?

While meditation teachers advise against constantly evaluating your meditation practice, you will naturally want to know if it's working, if you are on track. The benefits of meditation vary for individuals. Rather than judge each meditation session and whether it was a "good one," look to your daily life and work to see how it might be working. For example, do you feel calmer in situations that normally trigger the stress response? Do you feel more relaxed or energized following meditation practice? Are you more effective at work, getting more done with less stress? Do your relationships seem smoother, less tense? Are you more present-centered—living less in the past or the future? The meditation checklist (box 3.1) can be used if you are seeking a more detailed way to track progress.

BOX 3.1. MEDITATION PROGRESS CHECKLIST INDICATORS

___ I have noticed improved cognitive functioning (e.g., ability to concentrate when working/learning, memory seems enhanced, thinking is more fluid, creative solutions come easier).

___ I fall asleep quicker; my sleep also seems deeper, more refreshing.

___ My physical health seems better (e.g., fewer colds, less tense, fewer headaches, allergies improved).

___ I feel more comfortable with uncertainty and change.

___ My thoughts (in and out of meditation) seem more present-centered rather than based in the past (memories) or the future (planning).

___ I fall into meditation easier. It seems more natural and comfortable; I rely less on supportive tools, such as obsessing over whether I am focusing on the breath or mantra.

___ My meditation practice has become more of a priority; I find myself practicing consistently.

___ I am judging/evaluating myself less during meditation practice.

___ I find myself slipping into meditation states/moments more throughout the day.

___ Outside of meditation sessions, I notice my breathing more. I may also notice physical sensations in my body I previously didn't notice.

___ I am more aware of my thoughts and actions. There seems to be more "space," or a gap between when I think and take action. I feel like I have more choice in my response to the world around me.

___ I am more aware of my emotions, including when I begin to get angry.

___ I am enjoying simple pleasures more and feeling more connected to the environment. For example, I enjoy walking more, the morning cup of coffee, seeing the sunset or sunrise, hearing the birds chirp).

___ Others are noticing that I have changed (e.g., more relaxed, less reactive).

___ I am not annoyed or annoyed as often by things that normally bothered me (e.g., traffic jams, waiting in lines, comments by others).

___ I have stopped comparing my meditations (this was a "good" meditation; this was a "bad" one).

A MINDFULNESS-BASED MEDITATION METHOD: VIPASSANA

A commonly taught mindfulness meditation technique is *vipassana*, which is also known as insight or breath meditation. Rediscovered by the Buddha some 2,600 years ago, vipassana is described as a practical, secular meditation technique that can produce calm, peacefulness, and reduced stress (Vipassana Research Institute, n.d.). Vipassana relies heavily on mindfulness or present-moment awareness during the process of meditation. Combining "the best of both worlds" (Glickman, 2002, p. 40), vipassana draws upon both single-pointed focused and open-awareness-based methods. While there are different instructions for teaching vipassana, the following version is based on Glickman's (2002) instructions, which are based on the teachings of S. N. Goenka.

Sit comfortably, either on a chair or on a cushion on the floor. Your position should be "upright and comfortable," and one should feel "relaxed yet alert" (Glickman, 2002, p. 81). Point the chin slightly down and close the eyes or look down at an imaginary point about three feet in front of you. Allow the hands to relax on the legs, with palms facing up. Gently bring attention to the breath. "Breathing naturally, observe the sensations the touch of the breath makes in the area of the nostrils" (Glickman, 2002, p. 87). If the mind wanders and you are distracted by thoughts (this is completely natural and part of the process), simply return your awareness to the breath. You can experiment with focusing the attention on the temperature of the breath as it comes into nose (cooler air) and exits (warmer air). You can also focus awareness below the nostrils and above the upper lip. Another area of focus can be the navel, paying attention to how the belly rises and falls with the breath. Remember, regardless of where you place attention, avoid judging the experience or forcing anything to happen. The idea is to observe or witness the breath and, when becoming distracted, easily bringing awareness back to the breath.

Reading instructions on meditation may be difficult; thus, the following video-based guided vipassana meditations can be used to assist you, allowing you to follow along to the meditation teacher's voice.

- Jon Kabat-Zinn, 10-Minute Meditation: https://www.youtube.com/watch?v=2GjZanuXWWk
- Tara Brach, Guided Vipassana Meditation: https://www.youtube.com/watch?v=vbw0s_MoHOQ
- Jack Kornfield, Guided Insight Meditation: https://www.youtube.com/watch?v=bDEN7za1e5E

WHAT'S NEXT?

In the next chapter we will begin exploring the mindfulness-related attitudes or qualities, beginning with presence. We will examine how having a strong presence can enhance supervision.

Chapter Four

Presence in Supervision

While not one of the nine attitudes of mindfulness, presence is incredibly significant to the practice of mindfulness as well as supervision, teaching, and learning. *Presence* is "the underlying state that we access through mindfulness" (Hall, 2013, p. 43). The notion of presence has been called a "wide-awakeness" (Greene, 1973, p. 162) or, within the Buddhist tradition, "full awareness" (Mingyur Rinpoche, 2007, p. 940). While mindfulness and presence have been used interchangeably, they are not the same (Hall, 2013; Silsbee, 2016). Mindfulness is a route or vehicle to cultivate presence. Having presence means one is open, flexible, connected, and detached from the outcome. Helminski (2017) provides this skillful definition:

> *Presence* signifies the quality of consciously being here. . . . Presence is the way in which we occupy space, as well as the way we move and flow. Presence shapes our self-image and emotional tone. Presence determines the degree of our alertness, openness, and warmth. (pp. ix–xi)

Cultivating presence enables one to be more resilient and resourceful. For example, being present with others provides a sort of openness to "whatever is" occurring in the moment (Siegel, 2010). Through mindfulness-based practices, we gain a receptivity, an openness state unavailable to us when we are triggered by external stimuli and in a fight-flight-or-freeze response. Being present also means practicing *interpersonal mindfulness* (Duncan, Coatsworth, & Greenberg, 2009), which requires listening with full attention to others, present-moment awareness of emotions experienced by oneself and others during interactions, self-regulation of one's own emotions, and compassion for self and others. Presence also contains the practice of *deep listening*, or "a way of hearing in which we are fully present with what is happening in the moment without trying to control it or judge it" (Barbezat & Bush, 2014, p. 137). Deep listening is being present when listening but also bringing in acceptance and support (Silsbee, 2010).

In particular fields, such as nursing or counseling, where close, interpersonal interactions are required, presence becomes paramount (e.g., Hayes & Vinca, 2017; Melnechenko, 2003; Zyblock, 2010). In education, presence is perhaps equally important, but as Miller and Nigh (2017) note, presence is often missing from teacher education programs and curricula. Nevertheless, Noddings (2003) declared presence as fundamental to a caring relationship between teacher and student. For example, students can sense a teacher's presence—being completely attentive—or lack of it; and, as Miller and Nigh warn, "If we are continually distracted, we can lose a basic connection to our students" (p. 325). Rodgers and Raider-Roth (2006) describe: "Presence from the teacher's point of view is the experience of bringing one's whole self to full attention so as to perceive what is happening in the moment. . . . The image of an alert mind, ready to 'seize wholly,' in concert with a compassionate heart that stretches toward, ready to serve, captures much of what we mean by presence" (p. 267). Kessler (2000) asserts that "being fully alive to the present is the very 'heart of the teaching presence.'" For an educator, this means being open to perceiving what is happening right now and being responsive to that moment. It also means being flexible enough to "shift gears," using creativity to come up with a new approach and "being humble and honest enough to simply pause and acknowledge if a new approach has not yet arrived" (p. 9).

PRESENCE IN EDUCATIONAL SUPERVISION

Presence is equally essential in supervision, whether it's a principal coaching a teacher, a teacher assisting a colleague, or a university supervisor guiding a student teacher. While relatively little has been directly written about the concept within educational supervision, having presence is implied in a variety of aspects of supervision. To "bring out the best in teachers," in addition to technical skills, supervisors need a host of interpersonal skills, including listening, clarifying, encouraging, problem-solving, presenting, and negotiating—all of which *demand presence* (for more on this, see Glickman & Burns, 2020, pp. 57–58). The Developmental Approach to Supervision (Glickman, 1980), a well-known model for coaching teachers, requires educational leadership to either exercise more control and influence over aspects of the supervision process or give power to the teacher, depending on their level of development. Deciding on the appropriate level of control, no matter whether a supervisor sets the parameters for learning outcomes for students and how they will be measured or passes this responsibility to a teacher, relies very much on the educational leader being *highly present*. Determining the appropriate level of support requires being present throughout the entire supervision process. Take for example the Clinical Model, which, you recall, involves meeting with the teacher in advance to discuss the lesson, observing the teacher, collecting evidence of effective teaching, and post-conferencing to go over the results. During each stage, the supervisor must exercise intense presence to be successful in coaching a new or experienced educator. Not being fully present during a classroom observation, for instance, could mean a supervisor failing to collect sufficient or accurate evidence of teaching, which severely hinders the ability to provide authentic feedback and coaching.

CULTIVATING PRESENCE DURING THE CLINICAL SUPERVISION CYCLE

The following sections unpack how presence can factor into the stages of the clinical cycle (see table 4.1).

Pre-Conference

Pre-conferencing is considered by some to be the most important of the clinical stages (Sergiovanni & Starratt, 2007). During this stage, the supervisor must gain a conceptual understanding of the teacher's planned observation, seeing the lesson from the teacher's point of view as they mentally rehearse it before actually teaching. Thus, as a supervisor, you must be intensely present during these moments, listening attentively, knowing when to listen deeply and when to prod by asking guiding or clarifying questions. You cannot afford to miss a detail, a nuance, about the teacher's plans or thinking. Furthermore, an effective supervisor must sense the emotional atonement behind the sharing of the lesson, picking up on any signs of nervousness, doubt, or hesitation, which provide opportunities to provide support. Being present or fully alert with warmth and openness also creates the grounds for establishing a collaborative, supportive relationship between supervisor and supervisee. Just think of the opposite: a time when you tried to explain something to someone and they were distracted or not present (e.g., checking text messages on their cellular phone). How did that feel? What did it do to the relationship?

Table 4.1. Mindful Presence Informing the Clinical Cycle

Clinical Stage	Examples of Presence Needed
Pre-Conference	Consciously "being there" for the teacher
	Deeply listening
	Providing support and compassion
	Being alert, ready to shift gears
Classroom Observation	Being aware and "awake" for the lesson
	Fully noticing teachable moments
	Being open to the experience
Post-Conference	Same as noted for Pre-Conference

Classroom Observation

At the heart of the clinical model is the classroom observation, when the educational leader observes the teacher in action, watching "what the teacher actually says and does, how the students react, and what actually occurs during a specific teaching episode" (Sergiovanni & Starratt, 2007, p. 239). The supervisor also collects data in the form of observation notes, checklists, student work samples, or other evidence agreed upon during the pre-conference. As with conferencing, instructional leaders greatly benefit by being in a state of full awareness, completely in tune with what is unfolding in the classroom. Missing details—for example, what the teacher said specifically, how a student responded—could negatively impact the supervisor's ability to provide support and prompt growth and reflection during the post-conference. Not drifting mentally or getting distracted is critical when observing. Being able to bring yourself back or "return" your awareness to the present using mindfulness-based techniques (described later in this chapter) and developing the ability to hone in on teachable moments can prove very advantageous to supervisors.

Post-Conference

Maintaining presence is equally important when conferencing with a teacher after the observation. Being able to listen mindfully and respond fluidly in the moment as you support a teacher to reflect on a lesson and identify teachable moments and next steps is vital.

PRESENCE IN LEADERSHIP (SIX RESPONSE SKILLS)

Cultivating presence can also help support the practice of leadership skills, notably assisting education leaders *during* teaching. Let's look at how this quality supports each of the six immediate response skills.

Noticing

How can a supervisor notice a teachable moment if they are not fully aware of that moment? A profound moment, one that might be transformative for teacher learning, would likely slip right by. Being fully alert and responsive while in the classroom, observing and collaborating with the teacher, allows one to mentally identify teachable moments and record them as well.

Ignoring

Again, one must be fully conscious and open to all the possible teaching moments of a lesson to be in a position to decide which ones to intentionally "ignore" or put on hold for later conversations. One must also be in tune with the teacher, along with their emotions, stress levels, and challenges inside and outside the classroom, to know what teaching moments to ignore and what to pursue.

Intervening

Knowing exactly when to step in during a lesson or somehow support student learning as a supervisor requires intense presence and alertness. One must be extremely tapped into teachable moments, as intervening at the wrong time can have detrimental effects on teacher development and student learning.

Pointing

Emphasizing a teaching moment or providing real-time feedback demands present-moment alertness.

Processing/Unpacking

Helping a teacher understand and break down how a lesson went comes back to being fully present when interacting, as in conferencing mindfully.

A MINDFUL MOMENT

Take a moment to perform the following: Sit comfortably, close your eyes, and bring attention to your body, feeling any sensations or any tension. Allow each area of the body to relax. For instance, imagine directing your feet and ankles *to relax*, then do the same for your thighs and hips, your stomach, your chest, your neck and shoulders, and your face and head. Bring awareness to your breath, noticing how it also begins to relax. After a few minutes, slowly open your eyes and ask yourself, *Do I feel more present?* Learning to experience *relaxed awareness* can contribute to feeling and being more present in our lives and work.

MINDFULNESS-BASED PRACTICES TO DEVELOP PRESENCE

Hopefully, at this point in the chapter, you are convinced of the importance of cultivating a strong presence as an educational leader. The question then is: How do I develop presence? What are some specific ways mindfulness practices might help? The following section is devoted to providing specific methods and approaches to develop presence and connect it to your supervision practice. The various methods and techniques are organized by time commitment and level of difficulty, with those taking less time and practice presented first. Each method is also accompanied by a brief Supervision Context section to assist you in integrating the mindfulness practices into your work. Try out the methods that first interest you; give them perhaps a week or more, and see how they work. Mindfulness practices are highly personalized; thus, they require some experimentation.

The Mindful Minute

As the name implies, this technique, adapted from the work of Hall (2013), takes very little time. To practice the method, sit or stand comfortably. Keep the back straight but not stiff, firm but relaxed. Close your eyes if that's possible. Gently bring your awareness to your nostril area, noticing how the breath naturally flows in and out. Don't change the breath, for example, trying to deepen it. Simply observe it. If you have difficulty keeping awareness on the breath, you can count on the exhale—for instance, *one* as the breath leaves the nostrils, *two* as the breath again has come in and is going out. Observe the breath flow for one minute. Allow the awareness to move away from the breath, move the body if comfortable, and just experience whatever you are feeling.

Supervision Context

Since this technique is portable, you can practice anytime during your supervision routine. For example, you can engage in a Mindful Moment prior to pre-conferencing with a teacher or conducting a post-conference—in the process, strengthening your ability to be more present. In addition, you might complete the technique as you get ready to observe a teacher in the classroom, increasing your chances of teachable moments and gathering detailed evidence. The Mindful Moment can also be used *during* an observation or working with a teacher *during teaching* to bring one's awareness to the present. For example, practice this brief technique and experiment with how it impacts your ability to *notice* teachable moments.

Three-Minute Breathing Space

This method is also recommended by Hall (2013) and requires a small investment of time. This practice can be done anywhere, sitting or lying down. The technique starts with a wider perspective (a general check-in with your thoughts, feelings, and body), moving to a narrowing of awareness on the breath, then expanding out again to the whole mind-body and space around you. Begin with the eyes closed or gazing downward. During the first minute, ask yourself, *What are my thoughts? What are my feelings? What are my bodily sensations?* Do not force answers, just easily bring your awareness to these areas. In the second minute, gently shift your awareness to the in- and out-breaths, without changing the breathing. Just observe. During the last minute, widen your perspective, bringing awareness to the whole body, then the space around you; listen to any sounds, breathe in any smells. If the mind wanders during this practice, easily bring your awareness back without judgment.

Supervision Context

Like the Mindful Minute, the Three-Minute Breathing Space can be done at any time during the supervision process. A principal can engage in the practice prior to leaving their office to meet with a teacher or observe a lesson. A university supervisor, arriving at a partnership school to work with teacher candidates, can pause and practice awareness of thoughts, feelings, and the body, the breath, and the space around them, before leaving their car in the parking lot. A mentor teacher, collaborating with a colleague, can take three minutes in their classroom while students are at lunch or special gatherings. The idea is to work this practice into your daily routine so that it grounds you and regularly cultivates the quality of mindfulness. You can practice this method prior to observing teaching and see if you *notice* additional teachable moments, but also prior to reflecting on a list of teachable moments to determine what to ignore, point out, or help a teacher unpack.

Grounding in Mindfulness

Grounding exercises are used within the context of mindfulness to bring you back to the present moment. Since having presence is all about being in the present, a grounding technique called reorientation could help educational leaders in the midst of action bring themselves back to the moment. The technique works like this: Scan your environment, just taking it in. Take a few breaths. Identify five things you can see around you. No need to judge or define them, just allow your awareness to settle on them. Notice four things you hear around you—perhaps your breath, the humming of the air-conditioning, people talking. Just listen. Feel three objects around you. Maybe touch the fabric of your sweater, feel the shape of your cell phone, the desk or table, etc.

Smell two things. Simply breathe in and pay attention. Become aware of one thing you can taste. This means bringing awareness to your tongue and the taste buds. Do you taste "leftover" coffee, something from lunch, or nothing at all? After going through this process, you will likely feel more grounded in the present moment, no longer caught up in thoughts of all the tasks you have to do or something that happened in the past. Reflect on how this can boost your presence.

Supervision Context

You can use the Grounding in Mindfulness technique whenever necessary. If you begin to feel overwhelmed or distracted as you work with a teacher, for example, just start bringing awareness to the various senses, beginning with sight, moving to sound, etc. As an educational leader, you might need to do this to be present for a pre- or post-conference, when collecting data during an observation, or just interacting with a teacher. When gathering evidence during a lesson, looking for teachable moments, you might find focusing on your senses as you observe a teacher in action can help tremendously. Using this technique can assist in increasing alertness, openness, and in-the-moment responsiveness, aiding you in harmonizing with the teaching and determining whether to intervene or remain a bystander.

The Stage Exercise

This method of mindfully developing presence has been taught through the CARE for Teachers program as well as shared by faculty at Naropa University, a Buddhist-inspired institution in Boulder, Colorado. The Stage Exercise is normally done in front of a group of people, like in a classroom; however, this adaptation can be performed in front of a mirror at home. Keiser (2018), who uses this practice to help student teachers get comfortable standing in front of students, explains the exercise this way: You walk in front of the room, stop and breathe deeply to ground yourself, stand up straight, make eye contact with everyone in the group, then slowly walk off the "stage." If practicing alone, you could walk up to a mirror, intentionally stand tall, make eye contact, then slowly move away. To enhance this practice, be mindful of how it feels when you take a breath, when you make eye contact, and when you move slowly, more intentionally. Does it create a sense of presence by standing taller, for example?

Supervision Context

Bringing this practice into your supervision could mean rehearsing at home or in the privacy of your office, then being more aware of how you carry yourself when interacting with teachers. For example, when conferencing, pay attention to how you sit: Are you sitting up straight? Are you making appropriate eye contact as you listen to a teacher explain their lesson design or as you provide feedback? The Stage Exercise could help you be more present when you enter a classroom; maybe looking around, moving slower, breathing deeper. Experiment with it and see how it impacts various areas of your supervision.

Mindful Listening

As mentioned earlier in this chapter, deep listening is a fundamental component of presence and can greatly assist the supervision process. This mindful listening activity, adapted from the work of Barbezat and Bush (2014), requires a partner. The concept is to learn how to listen fully to the other person without judgment, interpretations, or interrupting, making them felt heard.

Begin with deciding who will be the speaker and who will be the listener. The speaker will talk for several minutes about a topic or prompt, expressing how they feel. For instance, they might discuss a lesson they recently taught or observed. The listener's job is to listen, to be curious but not ask questions. They can acknowledge the speaker through a gesture, such as nodding, but not speak during this time. Resist the urge to chime in or interrupt.

After the speaker has finished talking, the listener will paraphrase what they heard. The speaker can correct the listener if they misunderstood parts of the story. The listener can also attempt to describe what the speaker was "feeling" when they went through the experience.

When the speaker is satisfied that they were heard and comprehended, switch roles.

Supervision Context

Engaging in this mindful listening exercise can have tremendous benefit for a supervisor's ability to listen deeply during conferences or any time conversing with a teacher. Learning to listen with curiosity and care, withholding judgment or interpreting, can help build trust, connection, and create a space where feedback and constructivism criticism (delivered at a later time) will be received more positively. The ability to mindfully listen can also support assisting teachers in unpacking and reflecting on their pedagogical practices.

Becoming more present can have a powerful impact on your supervision practice. Engage with the above methods, seeing which ones you most resonate with, and what happens when you implement more than one.

WHAT'S NEXT?

In the next chapter we will begin exploring each of the attitudinal mindsets for cultivating mindfulness, starting with *beginner's mind*, and how they connect to supervision.

Chapter Five

Beginner's Mind in Supervision

Kabat-Zinn (2013) describes *beginner's mind* as "a mind that is willing to see everything as if for the first time" (p. 24). It is a mindset that perceives things as they are, free and uncluttered, before they become blocked by preconceived notions. The beginner's mind positions one to be responsive to whatever comes their way. With a beginner's mind, we avoid getting stuck or blocked by our own knowledge and expertise, able to capture the possibilities and wonder around us. Zen master Shunryū Suzuki (1970) famously captured the essence and benefits of this mindfulness-fueled state when he wrote:

> In the beginner's mind there are many possibilities, but in the expert's there are few. . . . The mind of the beginner is empty, free of habits of the expert, ready to accept, to doubt, and open to all possibilities. . . . When we have no thought of achievement, no thought of self, we are true beginners. Then we can really learn something. (pp. 13–14, 21–22)

Beginner's mind is highly transferable and can be applied to virtually any undertaking or profession (including educational supervision). Known as *shoshin* in Japanese, beginner's mind is evident in Japanese calligraphy, where the goal is to simply move the brush without embellishment, as "if you were writing for the first time" (Suzuki, 1970, p. 14). Within the art of dance, beginner's mind allows "each moment to be unique, and with an open mind can perceive the entirety of the moment with clarity. The mind is open—ready for anything" (Demerson, 2013, p. 99). Rather than discount accumulated experience or specialized knowledge, a beginner's mind practices with "with an opportunity to rejuvenate" and experience "heightened sensitivity" and "responsiveness to the present moment" (Demerson, p. 100).

Research suggests that society's norms enable experts in various fields to adopt close-minded, dogmatic orientations (Otatti et al., 2015). However, applying a beginner's mind can have positive results on the job. For example, novice software engineers were found to be more productive and innovative at certain tasks. "People tend to be more creative when they only partially understand a situation. Because they don't know all of the limits yet, they don't have as much difficulty seeing past them" (Belshee, 2005, n.p.). Applying Zen to grading papers, a law professor found that beginner's mind benefited students. "When I've achieved my goal in preparing the exam question, it also allows the student to exercise beginner's mind by expressing something fresh, original, and wonderful about policy, theory, and even well-established doctrine" (Robson, 2002, p. 313).

BEGINNER'S MIND AND EDUCATIONAL SUPERVISION

A Zen anecdote called "Cup of Tea" (Sensaki & Reps, 1957, p. 19) has often been used to illustrate the beginner's mind. As the story goes, a university professor visits a Japanese Zen master to inquire about Zen. While serving tea, the master intentionally pours the professor's cup until it's full then keeps pouring. Unable to restrain himself, the professor blurts, "The cup is full. No more will go in!" The master replies, "Like this cup, you are full of your own opinions and assumptions. How can I teach you Zen unless you first empty your cup?"

Approaching supervision with a beginner's mind means retraining one's perspective to see every facet with curiosity, freshness, and openness and awakening from being on autopilot. Each lesson described by a teacher, each classroom observation, is received with a sense of wonder. Preconceived notions of "good teaching" must be let go. Prior knowledge and experience do not prevent us from working with creativity and seeing possibilities. A specific example of a beginner's mind in the supervisory role is a principal, armed with years of teaching and administrative experience, sitting in a classroom, taking notes as he watches a second-grade teacher in action with her students. While he has perhaps observed dozens of teachers, the principal scripts the teacher's actions and words as if watching an elementary school lesson for the first time. He resists the urge to come to quick judgment or record only what teachable moments fit his teaching philosophy, based on what he taught in the classroom. Rather, he experiences the teaching in the present moment, hearing the sounds of the children talking in their small groups, seeing the teacher move about the classroom, reserving critical analysis for a later time.

The cultivation of a beginner's mind in supervision aligns well with inquiry-based supervision and practitioner research models, such as teacher inquiry and action research (see Glickman & Burns, 2020; Sergiovanni & Starratt, 2007). In inquiry-based supervision, the teacher and supervisor work together to identify a problem and work toward a solution. After the research is conducted, findings are shared and strategies for creating change are implemented. While inquiry-based approaches are not the focus of this book, this model certainly requires approaching problems in the classroom with openness, curiosity, and a strong spirit of inquiry. Likewise, the Clinical Supervision Model, which is built upon the idea of a coaching supervisor helping a teacher to practice, reflect, and grow, can be enhanced if those involved can set aside preconceptions and limitations caused by being an "expert."

CULTIVATING BEGINNER'S MIND DURING THE CLINICAL SUPERVISION CYCLE

The following sections address how the stages of the clinical cycle might be infused with a beginner's mind (see table 5.1).

Pre-Conference

Listening to a teacher's explanation of an upcoming lesson with openness and curiosity can be incredibly beneficial. Rather than judging or interrupting, the supervisor remains highly receptive to the teacher's plan, instead asking clarifying questions. With a beginner's mind, a supervisor might comment, "oh," "interesting," or "tell me more."

Classroom Observation

As explained, a supervisor exercising beginner's mind in the classroom still records evidence of effective teaching, but in the process immerses themselves

Table 5.1. Beginner's Mind During the Clinical Supervision Cycle

Clinical Stage	Examples of Mindful Attitude Practices
Pre-Conference	Approach the description of the teacher's planned lesson with curiosity. Ask questions. Remain receptive.
Classroom Observation	Observe with curiosity, wonder, and openness. Imagine you are watching a lesson being taught for the first time. How would you approach it?
Post-Conference	Put notes aside and listen with openness and curiosity. Allow yourself to be surprised by what you hear.

in the lesson with openness and wonder. The mindset of "I have seen this before" or "This is not the way math should be taught" must be cast aside in favor of an attitude of "What new strategies or teachable moments will I experience today?"

Data Analysis

During this stage, as you analyze the evidence collected through notetaking, rubrics, checklists, or other tools and prepare to share your findings with the teacher, you can approach this analysis with openness and curiosity and what is called "don't know" mind, or one that is free of opinions and comfortable with uncertainty. Go through the data, allowing yourself to be surprised, to question and wonder.

Post-Conference

Bringing a beginner's mind to discussions of how the lesson went can involve stepping out of your "expert" role and allowing the teacher to share insights and reflections. Together, you discover how the lesson went and collaborate to come up with next steps.

BEGINNER'S MIND AND THE IMMEDIATE RESPONSE SKILLS

The concept of beginner's mind can also inform the leadership response skills, particular ones that require open awareness in the present moment of teaching.

Noticing and Ignoring

Of the six leadership skills, noticing would be most influenced by cultivation of a beginner's mind. This mindset can powerfully transform how you spot teachable moments during instruction. You open your mind to many possibilities, many moments where teacher learning can occur, not allowing past experiences and preconceptions to limit what you recognize or list. Supervisors can also be open to their list of teachable moments, more receptive not only to what should be recorded and shared with teachers but also to what is intentionally ignored. The idea is to start with a blank slate, not bringing preconceived notions to the observation but rather remaining curious about what teachable moments might occur.

A MINDFUL MOMENT

After studying beginner's mind, take a few minutes and try the following exercise: Sitting somewhere with many details, such as a café or in the park, close your eyes or look downward and gently become aware of the breathing process, noticing how the breath naturally moves. Also notice that as the breath deepens, the body tends to relax. Then look around as if it's the first time you are seeing the environment, like a wide-eyed child entering a new place. Take everything in. Did you notice any new details? Did you see the environment from a new perspective?

MINDFULNESS-BASED STRATEGIES TO CULTIVATE BEGINNER'S MIND

There are various recommendations for developing a beginner's mindset, including simply asking questions to sitting meditation that involves contemplating what we don't know. Experiment with these exercises to find what works best to enhance your coaching of teachers.

Ask Questions

One of the most basic steps you can take in cultivating beginner's mind is to ask more questions. "Instead of operating on autopilot, question why certain tasks are completed in the ways you've normally done them" (MasterClass, 2022, n.p.). Trade conclusions and pre-established expectations for a spirit of inquiry.

Supervision Context

Create a list of "beginner's mind" questions that can be inserted into your current supervision procedures and routines. The questions in table 5.2 can be used when preparing for the pre-conference/post-conference or prior to or during a classroom observation.

Clear Your Mind

Try to empty your mind of preconceived notions or previous judgments before engaging in a task or studying a topic. You can use the Mindful Minute in chapter 3 or the Three-Minute Breathing Space method if time allows to help clear the mind and bring a freshness to what you are doing. If pressed for time, simply observing the breath might help you experience a feeling of openness.

Table 5.2. Beginner's Mind Questions for Conferencing and Classroom Observations

Routine Questions	"New" Questions
Does the lesson plan have all the required elements (e.g., learning objective, assessment, step-by-step plan)?	What different instructional planning design and innovative teaching strategies might I learn about today?
Does the teacher's explanation of the lesson fit or match my current view of "good teaching"?	What can I learn today about effective teaching?
Did the teacher properly assess student learning outcomes?	What new ways/ideas did the teacher share or plan regarding instructional assessment?
Has the teacher reflected and learned what I need them to learn?	What new insights and learning did the teacher uncover—things that might have surprised me as well?
Did the teacher meet "my" expectations with this lesson and performance?	What has this teacher "taught" me?
Is this lesson going well? Is the teacher teaching in a way I expect?	What's surprising me, making me wonder about this lesson as it unfolds? What am I noticing that I haven't noticed before?

Supervision Context

Clearing the mind through mindful breathing can be done prior to meeting with a teacher about their upcoming lesson. You can also engage in a Mindful Minute before stepping into a classroom to observe. Experiment with the possible connection between brief breath meditation exercises and beginner's mind.

Slow Down

According to Zen teachers and meditation instructors, slowing down your movements takes you off autopilot and encourages beginner's mind. By deliberately slowing your pace, you force yourself to experience each action or step of an activity more deeply. Also, slowing your pace causes you to remain in the present moment rather than focusing on the future.

Supervision Context

Intentionally slow the rate at which you would normally complete a supervision task. For example, if you are taking observation notes, deliberately slow the pace of your writing. As a result, you may write fewer notes, but you may begin to see the teaching and process of documentation with more clarity, openness, and a fresh perspective. Though time is always a challenge, you can also intentionally talk a little slower when conferencing or allow the teacher more time to talk, which will allow you to listen with a beginner's mind. Another idea is to just physically move slower throughout your workday. Try walking slower and more mindfully down the school hallway between classroom observations. See what happens to your mindset.

Become Fully Present to the Task at Hand

To experience beginner's mind, you can engage the senses to bring yourself more into the moment. The idea is to open your senses to experience something as if it's the first time you experienced it. For example, when engaged in a task, *What do you see? What colors become apparent? What shapes do you see? What patterns? What do you hear? Are these sounds close or far? What do you smell? Is it pleasant or unpleasant? What can you touch or feel around you? What is the texture?*

Supervision Context

Becoming fully present through the senses during supervision could mean observing a teacher, capturing evidence of teachable moments, and bringing awareness to what you see. Allow your eyes to fall on the colors in the classroom, the clothing of the teacher and students, the shape of the carpet near the rocking chair, the design of the bookshelf. Then shift to what you hear during the lesson: the teacher explaining directions with a patient (or frustrated) tone, the student asking to use the restroom, and the announcement coming over the intercom. Then become aware of the smell of cornflower from a recent science experiment, the air freshener in the corner of the room, etc. Focusing on the senses might create the curiosity needed to approach the observation with beginner's mind.

"Don't Know" Mind Meditation

This meditation, taught by mindfulness expert Jack Kornfield (2009), is a contemplation of all the things in the world that we don't fully understand and making peace with the idea that we can move through life without having all the answers. To practice this meditation: Begin by sitting comfortably with your eyes closed. Focus easily on the breath. Imagine your life 10 years in the future, recognizing that you don't know what will happen, where you will be, what you will be doing, and relax with that feeling. Consider some of the mysteries of life, Earth spinning through space, thousands of people born and dying each day, and how we don't really know how all these things are happening. Relax with this feeling. Now bring your mind to a problem or situation you face and think about how to be aware of all your thoughts and opinions about how things should be, how others should act. Now reflect on how we don't know if something that appears negative will lead to something better. Consider how it would feel to approach situations, people, or work with don't know mind. Feel it. You have no opinion, no fixed view. You have a sense of openness. How might this change or improve things? Practice this contemplation until you feel comfortable with not knowing, with uncertainty.

Supervision Context

After practicing this meditation, perhaps in the morning or prior to going to work, see if you can apply the feeling of don't know to various aspects of your supervision. For example, during pre-conferencing, relax with the feeling that you don't have to know everything the teacher will do during the observation in order to support them. Converse with the teacher, having no fixed opinion of how teaching "should be." Try this for a week and see how it impacts your role.

Mindful Eating

This activity can help promote beginner's mind by taking something we do every day, often on autopilot, and slowing down and bringing more awareness to the process. To engage in mindful eating, you can use any food, but it might help to use a single, smaller item, like a piece of fruit or chocolate. Hold the food in your hand as if you were seeing this food for the *first time*. Become aware of the texture, how it feels in your hand. Roll it around in your fingers, feeling the shape and contours. Bring the item to your nose, close your eyes, and deeply inhale. Be aware of how the smell impacts your mind and body. For instance, does it cause you to salivate or trigger childhood memories? Place the food in your mouth without chewing it. Just allow it to sit on the tongue, being aware of what happens to your taste buds. Intentionally chew the food slowly then swallow, being mindful of how the food moves down the throat toward the stomach. Sit with the eyes closed for a moment, paying attention to the body and your thoughts.

Supervision Context

You can practice mindful eating in this manner anytime. You can follow this more formal, thorough approach, but you can also bring awareness to eating—as well as drinking—at any time of the day. For instance, when sipping your morning coffee or tea, intentionally slow down, inhaling the aroma, paying attention to how this impacts your body. Sip fully and mindfully, immersing yourself in the sensation of the warm liquid moving down the throat. Pause and close your eyes. You can also practice mindful eating when enjoying a snack or lunch in between your supervisory responsibilities.

EXAMPLE OF BEGINNER'S MIND INFORMING THE CLINICAL CYCLE

Pre-Conference

Principal Warren prepares to meet with one of her fifth-grade teachers, Mrs. Stinson, to discuss an upcoming classroom observation science lesson. Prior to the meeting, the principal remains in her office, door closed, for a few minutes. Closing her eyes, she engages in a Mindful Minute, observing her breath and clearing her mind. She briefly contemplates how it's okay to not have all the answers, to feel the "don't know" mind. She has also prepared a brief list of beginner's mind questions for the conference, for example, "I wonder what new teaching strategies and ideas I will learn about today?" Intentionally moving slower, she takes a last sip of coffee and mindfully walks to the teacher's classroom, where the meeting is scheduled.

During the conference, she maintains openness and curiosity as she ensures that the teacher mentally rehearses and adequately explains her upcoming lesson. For instance:

> Principal Warren: "So tell me about your upcoming lesson? I'm curious!"
>
> Mrs. Stinson: "Well, I plan to teach the science standard requiring them to identify and understand the three classes of rocks."
>
> Principal Warren (thinking to herself): *I wonder how this standard can best be taught? How will she make it engaging for students?*

Classroom Observation

Prior to heading to Mrs. Stinson's classroom, Principal Warren uses the Three-Minute Breathing Space to center herself. She intentionally slows her steps on the way to the school's fifth-grade hallway, remembering that to avoid operating on autopilot, she can slow her movements. To encourage a beginner's mind, Warren has jotted down a few questions on her data collection tool, including *I wonder what will surprise me today during this lesson?* During the observation, to become fully present, she focuses on her sense of sight, taking in all the shapes and colors of the classroom, then shifts awareness to the sounds around her.

Post-Conference

Like when preparing for the pre-conference, Principal Warren practices a Mindful Minute before the teacher arrives at her office. In her notes she has written a guiding question: *"What new insights and ideas will I learn from this teacher today?"* She engages Mrs. Stinson with curiosity and openness, setting aside the impulse to judge, correct, or interrupt. For example:

> Principal Warren: "So tell me more about how your use of the Nearpod technology enhanced learning in your opinion? I'm curious to learn more about this tool."
>
> Mrs. Stinson: "I think the tech tool engaged the students through the interactive videos and enabled me to formatively assess them in real time."

WHAT'S NEXT?

In chapter 6 you will study how the mindful attitudes of patience and trust can inform supervision.

Chapter Six

Patience and Trust in Supervision

In this chapter we will explore how the mindfulness attitudes of *patience* and *trust* can factor into our work with teachers. For the purpose of this writing, the term "patience" is defined as understanding and accepting that "sometimes things must unfold in their own time" (Kabat-Zinn, 2013, p. 23), while "trust," in the context of mindfulness, can be defined as relying on and honoring one's own intuition and feelings rather than always looking "outside of yourself for guidance" (Kabat-Zinn p. 25).

Patience, as explained by Kabat-Zinn (2013), "is a form of wisdom" (p. 23). Possessing this quality, we realize that things must often happen in their own time and that interfering can hurt or delay this process. The classic example used is the child who thinks they are helping a butterfly to grow by breaking its chrysalis, not understanding that this process cannot be rushed. When learning mindfulness or practicing meditation, we learn to be patient with our minds and bodies, allowing various experiences to unfold and realizing that the mind may judge or become agitated, questioning whether our practice is helping or why aren't things happening faster. With patience, we give ourselves permission to make mistakes, for room to stumble, reflect, and grow.

According to Schnitker (2012), there are three types of patience: (1) daily hassles, such as traffic jams, long lines, or no internet connection; (2) interpersonal, when others cause us frustration or suffering; and (3) life hardship, which might include dealing with mental or physical illness, systematic racism, or other long-term suffering. Being patient has its benefits. Research suggests that those with patience experience less depression and negative emotions and are more cooperative, empathetic, and productive (Schnitker & Emmons, 2007; Schnitker, 2012). The good news is that patience, like a muscle, can grow through use. We can learn to breathe and wait in line at the grocery store or coffee shop drive-thru more calmly. We can become more patient when striving for goals, knowing that the bigger the goal, the more time it will likely take. We can become more patient with family, friends, and co-workers, allowing room for them to speak and be heard and to make their own mistakes. Part of developing patience, however, is tempering our impulse control and learning to practice delayed gratification in a culture of instant gratification—e.g., online purchasing, instantly streaming movies and shows, food delivery services (Smith, 2021).

Several factors impact the development of patience (Grossman et al., 2009). First is personality; people with higher levels of agreeableness and conscientiousness tend to be more patient, as do individuals who are more optimistic and feel they have a greater sense of control over their life. As we age, we can also become more patient, perhaps due to gaining greater long-term perspective. Mindfulness meditation appears to be one of the most effective ways to increase patience, as it enhances attentional control, emotional regulation, and cognitive flexibility (Tang et al., 2010). Later in the chapter, we will explore some mindfulness meditation methods that support the development of patience.

PATIENCE IN EDUCATIONAL SUPERVISION

Supporting teachers, whether they are currently working in the classroom or preparing to enter the profession, demands patience and trust. Every stage of the clinical model, for instance, requires patiently guiding a teacher as they learn to improve student learning. To better understand the significance of patience within supervision, looking outside the clinical model for a moment to another prominent supervision approach, the Developmental Model, might help. The Developmental Model, first proposed by Glickman (1980) and revised through the years, posits that supervisors need to be keenly aware of the developmental needs of teachers they work with and, based on those needs, operate from one of three orientations: *(1) nondirective, (2) collaborative,* or *(3) directive.* Within these orientations, supervisors enact various behaviors to support teachers, including listening, clarifying, encouraging, and problem-solving. For example, after observing a third-grade teacher struggling with classroom management, a supervisor would take a more directive approach by delineating clear standards of performance and creating a timeline of teacher actions to be completed. Using a collaborative approach, on the other hand, a supervisor might notice that a teacher is struggling less with student behaviors but is constantly in motion and appears tired and worn down by her teaching. The supervisor in this case might discuss the problem and, in a friendly manner, negotiate some actions that the teacher might take—perhaps not staying up so late to plan lessons and placing more responsibility on students to manage materials in the classroom. Finally, in the nondirective orientation, the supervisor realizes that the teacher identifies their own instructional problems and seeks solutions. In this situation, the supervisor serves mainly as a facilitator, with less formality, perhaps using only portions of the five clinical stages.

You can see that high amounts of patience are necessary, particularly when a teacher requires more directive supervision. While taking a more involved approach, a supervisor would do well to remember that this teacher must develop *in their own time*, as much as the supervisor may wish the development to occur faster. The teacher must undergo the necessary experiences, reflection, and corrective action to progress and gain competency. In this case, the teacher very much symbolizes the butterfly in the chrysalis, requiring the right amount of time to emerge and flourish. The supervisor will only hurt the teacher's growth by pushing too hard or being impatient. They must exercise the wisdom to know when to expect more and the right amount of push and direction. Additionally, the supervisor must trust that the teacher can and will grow in their own time. They must also trust that the process—the cycle of conferencing, observing, analyzing, and conferencing with feedback—will ultimately work.

TRUST AND INTUITION

Trust, in the context of cultivating mindfulness, asks us to trust our own intuition and feelings. When it comes to learning meditation, Kabat-Zinn (2013) advises that it is better to trust one's intuition and own authority, even if some mistakes are made, than to always look to the outside for guidance and affirmation. Trust requires honoring basic feelings, and knowing you possess basic goodness and wisdom. Rather than try to emulate someone else, you learn through mindfulness training to listen and trust your own being.

To tap into intuition, however, you must practice stilling the mind and calming the constant mental chatter. Mindfulness meditation nourishes our relationship with ourselves, deepening the connection and making it easier to tune into your own feelings about people and situations. Before proceeding to enhance our intuition through mindfulness, an explanation of *intuition* is needed. Intuition has been considered a mysterious phenomenon. Research is relatively thin on the concept of intuition (and arguments persist even over its existence). Various models and definitions of intuition have been proposed, such as Koestler's notion that the act of intuition is generally conceived as a "moment of truth" or "sudden emergence of a new insight." As Baylor (1997) explains, intuition is in play when a "clinical psychologist initiates a new direction in therapy by deciding to confront her client at just the right time" or a "neuropsychologist sees a connection between his research and a colleague's cognitive psychological model, leading him to implement a new set of methods and add a meaningful new dimension to his research" (p. 185). For a principal, intuition might be knowing when to capture a teachable moment or step in during an observation when a student is in physical danger.

One theory of intuition is that it is an unconscious process, happening below the level of conscious awareness (Stanovich & West, 2008). In this sense, intuition provides us with a kind of "mental shortcut," enabling us to more quickly process information and make decisions based on past experiences. Another theory is that intuition is a type of emotional intelligence, or the ability to comprehend and interpret emotions (Mayer & Salovey, 1997).

The Two Minds model (see table 6.1) provides another theoretical framework to better understand intuition and how it acts in our lives. The theory posits that our minds have evolved into "two minds": a reasoning, analytical mind, and a more primitive "intuitive mind" responsible for feelings and behaviors (Sadler-Smith, 2007, 2010). The reasoning mind is harnessed in school and formal education, giving us the ability to reason and problem-solve. This more recently evolved mind communicates to us in easily understood language: words. However, the Two Minds theory asserts that we have a more ancient mind, which likely developed as a "neurobiological alarm bell" that served as an early warning system for danger, helping us to decide what do to in each moment to survive, who to trust, what to avoid, etc. Unlike the analytical mind, the intuitive mind does not communicate with words in our conscious awareness but rather speaks a different language in the form of a "gut feeling" or "hunch." This intuitive function is sometimes referred to as our "sixth sense."

Both minds are needed to function effectively in daily life; however, nurturing the intuitive mind can enhance our ability to make important, complex

Table 6.1. The Two Minds Descriptors

Analytical Mind	Intuitive Mind
Narrow mental bandwidth	Broader mental bandwidth
Conscious-processes, open to direct introspection	Unconscious-processes, not open to direct introspection
Communicates in language of "words"	Communicates in language of "feelings"
Slower operation	Faster operation
Evolution more recent (perhaps tens of thousands of years old)	Evolution ancient (perhaps hundreds of thousands of years old)

Note: Adapted from *The Intuitive Mind: Profiting from the Power of Your Sixth Sense* (Sadler-Smith, 2010)

social, moral, and professional decisions when not all the facts are available and time is limited. For example, in the case of educational supervision, decisions that impact teachers' instructional practices and student learning must often be made with immediacy.

Hence, if one subscribes to theories of intuition, and the idea of having intuitive hunches, the next question becomes: *How do I develop or strengthen that ability?* Mindfulness meditation methods, by training our minds to focus on the present moment, make us more aware of our thoughts and emotions (Tang et al., 2010). Mindfulness practice has also been linked to greater levels of emotional intelligence (Neff, 2003). At first glance, mindfulness, considered a conscious cognitive function, and intuition, a nonconscious cognitive function, may appear to be contradictory. However, a closer look reveals the two to be highly complementary. Mindfulness not only involves present-moment awareness—for instance, of what is occurring in one's environment—but also, according to mindfulness teachers such as Kabat-Zinn, is primarily concerned with awareness of one's thought process, emotions, and actions. Dane and Pratt (2009) also assert that mindfulness expands past definitions of present-moment awareness of events but also covers the cognitive and emotional process occurring within an individual. While limited literature on the topic has reported mixed findings on the relationship between mindfulness and intuitive problem-solving (see Remmers et al., 2015; Zedelius & Schooler, 2015), Brown and Ryan's (2003) research found a positive relationship between mindfulness and a deeper connection between explicit and implicit emotions, suggesting that mindfulness could trigger access to nonconscious phenomena such as intuition. When studying the management styles of business executives who meditate, McNaughton (2013) found that they relied on intuition when making a majority of their decisions.

INTUITION AND SUPERVISION

In the field, educational supervisors could benefit from learning to tap into their intuitive function, learning to balance analytical decision-making with more trust in feelings and hunches about good teaching. It could be argued that supporting and coaching teachers, like teaching itself, is more an art—a feel—than a science, where certain actions create probable results. As a principal, assistant principal, university supervisor, or mentor teacher/colleague, we are with individuals who have different temperaments, backgrounds, talents, and abilities. No one approach will work for all teachers. Supervisors must be attuned to when things feel right—and when they don't—and learn to act on those hunches. Practicing various mindfulness techniques and learning to meditate make one more aware of intuition's inner language. Despite stronger levels of intuition, supervisors are not advised to completely discard analytical thinking as they conduct an observation and gather data, for example.

The use of intuition when supervising teachers has been hinted at in the literature. In his work on educational supervision, drawing from Carl Jung's writings, Pajak (2003) theorized that supervisors exercise four psychological functions of perception, which influence how they observed a classroom lesson. Individuals perceive experiences mainly through one of the psychological lenses: thinking, sensing, feeling, or *intuiting*. An intuitive supervisor might observe the same lesson but focus more on abstract phenomena such as theories, ideas, and future possibilities and have "spontaneous leaps of imagination and may omit or neglect details" (p. 13). Thus, Pajak encouraged supervisors to strive to more fully develop all four functions to become more whole and effective in their work.

CULTIVATING PATIENCE AND TRUST DURING THE CLINICAL SUPERVISION CYCLE

As shown in table 6.2, mindfully cultivating patience and trust and accessing intuition can enhance conferencing and observations. Let's look more closely and how these qualities might inform the different stages.

Pre-Conference

When meeting with teachers, this is an opportune time to bring patience to the process. Depending on their developmental stage, educators may be nervous when explaining their lesson plans and pedagogy to a supervisor. Some may be highly skilled and talented in the classroom with students but struggle to articulate their plans and goals. Others may need guidance on designing teaching components such as pacing, classroom management, and assessment. This can also be a time to listen to your intuition, relying on any feelings or hunches you may experience as you hear a lesson described, guiding you in real time to make decisions about when to clarify, question, or simply listen to a teacher.

Classroom Observation

We can practice patience mindfully during classroom observations, when we might expect to see a teachable moment. While holding teachers to high standards, we must remind ourselves that we all have good and bad teach-

Table 6.2. **Mindful Patience and Trust Informing the Clinical Stages**

Clinical Stage	Examples of Mindful Attitude Practices
Pre-Conference	Be patient as you listen to a teacher's planned lesson. Understand their development level and their current challenges in their role.
	Trust your intuition to guide you in coaching the teacher. Pay attention to your feelings about when to speak and when to listen.
Classroom Observation	Practice patience during the observation, reminding yourself that things must unfold in their own time. If you do not see "highly effective" teaching or student learning in that moment, it does not mean you will not see it later.
	Take intuitive notes, writing down teachable moments that move you and resonate.
Post-Conference	Be patient and understanding, even if a teacher is not highly reflective of their teaching or responsive to feedback. Allow space for this to happen.

ing days, that high performance is not always a guarantee, and that teaching is an incredibly demanding craft. When watching a lesson, supervisors can also stay attuned to gut feelings as a lesson unfolds: What "feels right" in the teaching? What "feels off"?

Post-Conference

Meeting with the teacher after the observation to discuss how it went and whether student learning outcomes were achieved provides another opportunity to be patient in listening and understanding. Perhaps the teacher might have an unrealistic view of how the lesson went or need support in understanding how to analyze student work to determine if the lesson was effective and the next steps. During this time, as supervisors we can pay attention to any feelings or hunches about when to provide additional support, structure, or guidance and how best to encourage reflection on practice.

PATIENCE AND TRUST AND THE IMMEDIATE RESPONSE SKILLS

Noticing

When engaging in supervisory leadership skills, we must be patient when "waiting" for teachable moments. As Kabat-Zinn reminds us, things often need space to unfold in their own time. Effective teaching cannot be rushed.

Also, when collecting observational data, pay attention to feelings as you notice teachable moments. When something jumps out at you or stirs you, there is a reason. Write it down to discuss with the teacher during conferencing. Trust that this moment in the classroom resonated, whether it was something particular a student said, the way students put away their supplies and materials, or the tone of the teacher's voice when redirecting a student.

Ignoring

When deciding what not to focus on during an observation or record in your notes, the intuitive mind can serve a supervisor well. Observing and data collection require a sense of immediacy; there is no time to think about whether there is a teachable moment to list or emphasize. Thus, lean on your intuitive feelings and gut to *know* when a moment is significant in the classroom and warrants further discussion.

Intervening

Perhaps mindful patience and cultivated intuition can play the biggest role in this skill. As a supervisor, you may want to jump in every moment and save the students or guide or correct the teacher in how they are teaching fractions or the life cycle. This requires hanging back, trusting the process, and giving the teacher space and time to teach, reflect, and grow. On the other hand, a principal, for instance, must intuitively respond immediately if a student appears in danger or a teacher makes a disparaging or harmful remark to a student.

MINDFULNESS-BASED PRACTICES TO ENCOURAGE PATIENCE AND TRUST

There are a number of ways to cultivate patience and trust in one's feelings and intuition. As in other chapters, the exercises are presented from least-intensive to most time-consuming.

The Bell Exercise

This simple mindfulness activity can begin to build patience (Smith, 2021). You will need a meditation bell, a chime, a guitar string, or a similar device to create a sustained tone. Sit comfortably; make the sound then focus on the tone until you hear it completely stop. Continue the exercise, making the sound a little louder each time to sustain the note. This will extend your focus and attention. Note: This is also a great way to warm up the mind for sitting meditation.

Supervision Context

Practice the Bell Exercise at home, outside of work, then see if you bring that mindful patience to different situations when supervising. For instance, when listening during conferences, you can "listen" to the teacher like the bell sound, gently keeping your focus on their words, their tone, and the emotion behind their communication.

Counting the Breath

This exercise will build patience by using awareness of the breath and the frequency of thoughts during the process of meditation. Sit comfortably in a quiet place. As you observe your breath, count to yourself on the out-breath. For instance, you watch the breath go in and, as you exhale, silently say to yourself, *one*. Continue to count toward 10. Any time you have a thought or become distracted (likely in the beginning), gently start over, beginning with the count of one.

Supervision Context

Bring the sense of "returning" focus during your role as supervisor, such as becoming distracted when speaking with a teacher or collecting data during an observation. In addition, you use the breath to anchor yourself and practice anytime, anywhere. When feeling frustrated, for example, return awareness to the flow of the breath. You can silently count the breaths or add a phrase such as "calm" as the breath goes in or out.

Wrist Malas

Mala beads have been around for thousands of years, with origins in India and Nepal. Made from plant seeds, wood, or animal bone, the beads are used to form jewelry and aid in the meditation process. The beads provide something tactile to help maintain focus on the breath or a mantra. Malas typically come in necklace form, with 108 beads representing various spiritual teachings. Mala bracelets (see figure 6.1), with as few as 18 beads, are ideal for "mobile" meditation aids. Using malas for meditation does not require spiritual beliefs or non-secular practices.

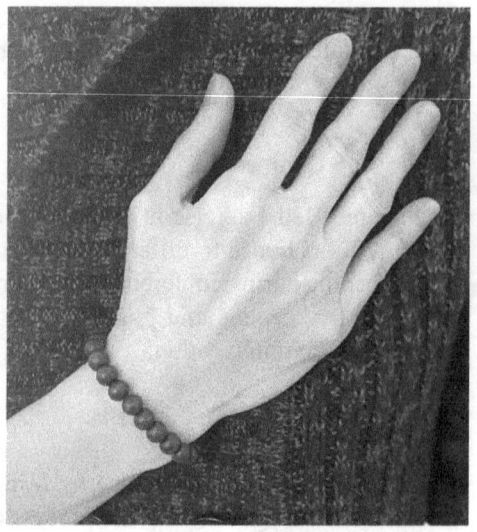

Figure 6.1. Meditation Mala Beads
Photo courtesy of author

To use the mala bracelet to help build mindfulness and patience, begin with the bracelet in your left hand, with your index finger and thumb gently holding a bead as pictured in figure 6.2. Move the beads through your fingertips, one by one, focusing on the breath or a mantra—for example, saying "calm" or "one" as you move a bead. Continue to do this with each bead, completing the whole bracelet if possible.

Figure 6.2. Using Mala Beads
Photo courtesy of author

Supervision Context

Malas can be used to help with sitting meditation; for example, using them during a mindfulness meditation session in the morning. However, you can bring them into your supervision role by wearing the mala bracelet (they also make a nice fashion statement) and, whenever the need arises, moving the beads while focusing on the breath. Maybe you are waiting for a teacher to begin an observation lesson and want to be more present. Simply, mindfully move the beads. Another application could be meditating with the malas when you feel overwhelmed by supervisory responsibilities or are about to interact with a teacher regarding a tense topic.

Body Scan Meditation

Another mindfulness meditation involves mentally scanning the body. Knowing the body, including its sensations and responses, at a deeper level can become a tremendous ally in developing patience as well as tapping into intuition. The body scan, which can be done sitting comfortably or lying down, involves systematically and mentally scanning the body with your awareness. Practicing the body scan enables one to become more in tune with bodily sensations, both pleasant and unpleasant, and more aware of how tension and the stress response are experienced in the body. When we grow impatient, for example, what happens in the body? Do you feel tension in a certain place? Do you clench your fists, does the stomach tighten, do the shoulders tense and come up? These subtle cues can communicate to us when we are triggered and need to step away, focus on our breathing, and take other steps to regulate the nervous system. Tuning into the body also cultivates intuition by increasing awareness to the language of gut feelings and hunches, which arise within the body. We might feel a tightening in our stomach when entering a situation with a teacher or have a feeling of lightness when a solution comes to us about how to handle a supervision scenario. Practicing the body scan might increase receptivity to such experiences.

Begin the body scan method by bringing awareness to the top of the head, sensing into the area, just observing the sensations that already exist. Gently move your awareness to the forehead, feeling into the region. Continue moving the attention down through the eyes, nose, and mouth to the jaw. If you notice tension in a particular area, don't try to relax or make anything happen. Just be aware of what is happening without judgment. Become aware of the shoulders, then scan down the arms through the triceps, biceps, and forearms, settling into the hands, sensing into the muscle tissue. Feel the energy that circulates through the fingers and the palms.

Scan back up through the arms to the chest area, becoming aware of any sensations around the heart. Move awareness through the sternum to the abdomen. Bring awareness to the hips and buttocks then the thighs, sensing into each area, perhaps feeling a sense of heaviness. Finally, bring the awareness down through the calves, ankles, and into the feet. Allow your mind to work through the soles, the toes, feeling the energy. Complete the meditation by experiencing the body as a whole, allowing the mind to pick up any sensations (e.g., pain, aches, tingling, tension, relaxation, lightness, heaviness) that arise. When ready, slowly open your eyes.

Abridged Body Scan

If pressed for time, you can try this condensed version of the body scan awareness practice: Begin by sitting in a comfortable posture, closing your eyes, and observing your breath. Bring awareness to the neck and shoulders, noticing any tension. After about 30 to 45 seconds, bring awareness to the heart area. Move your awareness to the soles of the feet. Finally, become aware of the palms. Return your attention to the flow of the breath; when ready, open your eyes.

Supervision Context

While the body scan can become part of your mindfulness practice, engaging the method perhaps in the morning and also before going to sleep, educational supervisors can bring the benefits of bodily mindfulness to their roles at school by listening to how the body reacts in various situations. During classroom observation, supervisors can "listen" to their bodies, knowing when a particular teaching moment "feels right" or doesn't. This intuitive approach can then inform what teaching moments you emphasize when conferencing or what you let go. Practicing body scan meditation can also make one more aware of the conditioned responses associated with their role. For example, do you "push away" from certain conversations with teachers (e.g., classroom management was a disaster; the lesson didn't make sense; the content taught was inaccurate) or cling to certain situations or teachers (e.g., I really enjoy watching this teacher in action; I love how this teacher reflects deeply on their lessons). Becoming more cognizant of these unconscious reactions provides space to make new, more-empowered choices.

Loving-Kindness Meditation

Loving-Kindness, another Buddhist-based meditation practice, can also help strengthen the quality of patience and attunement to inner feelings and responses. Loving-Kindness Meditation requires one to send feelings or "vibes" of loving kindness to oneself and others from a meditative state.

Begin by sitting comfortably and closing your eyes. Become aware of the breath for a few minutes, then shift the awareness to the heart area. Imagine a benefactor—someone who brings you happiness and joy just being in their presence. This individual can be someone deceased or even a pet. (*Note:* This person or being should elicit a positive response; avoid bringing up an individual that produces feelings of grief, loss, or other negative emotions.) See them sitting before you, smiling; picture their face if possible. Now, imagine the feelings you would experience in their presence. Allow those feelings to saturate your body, your being. Then, on each out-breath, very gently repeat a mental phrase such as "may you be happy" or "may you be well" and imagine that an energy of loving kindness is flowing from your heart to theirs. You can imagine this loving-kindness energy positively impacting them, perhaps causing them to feel calmer or even smile. When ready, return awareness to the breath then slowly open your eyes. This method is sometimes taught by using yourself as the object of loving kindness, though this can be difficult for some people. Also, after practicing the technique with a benefactor, one can gradually move toward imagining sending loving-kindness vibes to a "neutral," someone they perhaps see in the community (the grocery store, at work, etc.) but don't know personally. To really strengthen one's loving-kindness muscles, the method can also be directed toward a difficult person, someone you may have had an argument with or has harmed you on some level, but this is not advised without guidance and experience.

Supervision Context

Loving-Kindness Meditation can also be practiced in private but directed toward one's supervision. For example, try sending loving kindness to a teacher or team of teachers you are currently supervising, generating positive emotions and increasing patience. In time, you could level-up your practice to generating loving kindness for a struggling teacher or one challenging your patience.

EXAMPLE OF PATIENCE AND TRUST (INTUITION) INFORMING THE CLINICAL CYCLE

Pre-Conference

Principal Warren prepares to meet with one of her fifth-grade teachers to discuss an upcoming classroom observation social studies lesson. That morning, Warren woke 10 minutes earlier and practiced counting her breath to develop focus and patience and spent a few minutes engaging in a Loving-Kindness Meditation, sending positive vibes to various teachers, including Mrs. Stinson, who she would observe later in the day.

During the conference, Principal Warren returns focus to her breath if she feels the urge to jump in or impose her teaching beliefs on Mrs. Stinson. She listens mindfully and deeply to Mrs. Stinson describe her social studies lesson, remembering that she is still partially in a *directive* stage of supervision, requiring more guidance on elements such as crafting her student learning objective and assessment. However, Principal Warren also listens to her body, noticing when and where she might tense up when hearing certain information or words. She tunes into whether aspects of the lesson planning "feel right" and if she should interject or remain quiet.

Classroom Observation

During Mrs. Stinson's classroom observation, Principal Warren becomes aware that she is growing impatient that the teacher has not addressed the disruptive behavior of two students in the back of the room. Warren tries to breathe mindfully but needs additional support, so she discreetly holds the mala bracelet she is wearing and slowly moves a few beads while counting her breaths. Of course she has noted the students' behavior—which continued to decline and impact nearby students—as a teachable moment to be addressed when conferencing, but Warren intuitively decides (she goes with her gut feeling) that Mrs. Stinson requires some grace in further developing her classroom management skills; interjecting herself into the lesson as principal would not help matters.

Post-Conference

In her office prior to the post-conference, Principal Warren performed a brief body-awareness scan, noticing some tension in her shoulders and neck. She also felt somewhat uneasy about the upcoming conference with Mrs. Stinson, so she listed some points she wanted to make and considered how to phrase them. When talking with Mrs. Stinson, Warren struggled with holding back about the students' misbehavior as she waited for the topic to be brought up as a point of reflection. As Warren began to address the topic, she sensed a stressful energy and noticed that Mrs. Stinson became emotional. With teary eyes, the teacher began to express the extreme stress she had been under both personally and professionally. At this point, Warren went with her intuitive feelings and, after caringly listening, informed Mrs. Stinson that it would be best to reschedule the post-conference to a later time.

WHAT'S NEXT?

In the next chapter we will entertain the ideas of letting go and non-striving within the context of supervision work.

Chapter Seven

Letting Go and Non-Striving as a Supervisor

Letting go is a concept with roots in Taoism and Buddhism. The idea of letting go means accepting things in the moment, as they are, as they unfold, without resistance. Letting go is often more accurately described as "let it be." To the Western mind, the concept of letting go is often mistaken for passivity—or simply accepting what happens without taking action or the ability to change things. Rather, letting go and non-striving in the context of mindfulness means being present with experiences, not resisting what we cannot currently change; conserving energy, but also remaining open, flexible, and responsive to take effective action when the time is right. By letting go, one acts completely in the moment, without attachment to a particular outcome or expectation.

To better understand the concepts of letting go and non-striving and provide context, some background on Taoism is necessary. Taoism is one of the world's oldest religions and philosophies, dating back to the first millennium BCE. Taoism teachings are found in classics such as the *Tao Te Ching*, in which famed teacher Lao Tzu extrapolates on the principles and concepts of the Tao, or "Way." In these texts, the Tao "is the unifying, unseen, yet ever present force that governs the universe. With no beginning or end, the Tao in its essence represents the universal undifferentiated state beyond the laws of duality that control our physical existence" (Glanz, 1997, p. 195). The basic idea is to flow with the Tao rather than resist. Like the current of a river, one can move more easily with it as opposed to swimming upstream. In Taoism this is described as *wu wei*, or the idea of least action. This doesn't mean we do nothing; rather, it's the use of gentle force or expending less energy but still getting results.

However, this idea of least resistance also requires letting go, releasing limiting thoughts or memories, dropping emotional baggage, or cutting out people or possessions so one can move more freely in the present moment. As mindfulness teacher Jack Kornfield (2023) explains, "Letting go does not mean losing the knowledge we have gained from the past. The knowledge of the past stays with us. To let go is simply to release any images and emotions, grudges and fears, clingings and disappointments that bind our spirit. Like emptying a cup, letting go leaves us free to receive, refreshed, sensitive, and awake" (n.p.).

The following Zen Buddhism story illustrates the practice of letting go in daily life.

A senior monk and a novice monk come upon a woman who is trying to cross a river. The senior monk, seeing she needs help, picks her up and brings her across the water. Setting her down safely, he continues walking. A few hours later, the novice, disturbed by the incident, questions the senior monk: "We took a vow not to come in physical contact with a woman? How could you do that?" The senior monk looks at his traveling companion and simply says, "I left the woman behind at the river. Apparently, you have not."

Letting go is fundamental to practicing mindfulness (Kabat-Zinn, 2005). When paying attention to our inner experience—for example, during sitting meditation—we soon learn that we have thoughts and feelings and past events we want to retain. Generally, our instinct is to cling to pleasant thoughts and sensations while pushing away unpleasant ones. However, mindfulness practice strengthens our ability to override the tendency to cling to or push away experiences. When we find ourselves judging experience (and we naturally will), we practice letting go of those judging thoughts. We intentionally let go of those impulses. Likewise, when thoughts of past or future tense arise, we let them go; as Kabat-Zinn (2005) says, "We just watch." Using mindfulness, even if something becomes difficult to let go, we can bring awareness to what strong "holding on" feels like. In time, we grow more skilled in recognizing our attachments.

Letting go as a mindful practice is not the same as *aversion*, which is moving away from something we dislike, hate, or fear. Aversion is a survival mechanism built into our evolution-drive brains, keeping us away from things that could be harmful (Hanson, 2009). But healthy letting go looks more like intentionally releasing something (e.g., negative emotion, unhealthy habit), saying goodbye to thoughts, emotions, situations, or people that are unwholesome for our lives rather than subconsciously avoiding something, which can trigger the fight-flight-or-freeze response or cause us to act impulsively or negatively toward others.

Naturally, when learning to let go of attachment and embracing non-striving, you might be concerned about losing motivation and drive when approaching goals with an attitude of letting go. However, pursuing goals with nonattachment could increase effectiveness and remove much of the stress that comes with accomplishment. The idea is to find the sweet spot between moving toward what we want and not becoming rigid or attached in the process (see the Intention and Attachment Matrix, figure 7.1). Having *high intention* toward an outcome means we give it energy and advance in that direction. However, if we do so with *high attachment*, we become too narrow in our vision and fixed on that outcome happening a certain way. Thus, we may greatly limit the possibilities of how we may hit the target. In the case of supervision, this might mean coaching several struggling teachers to improve and find their rhythm in the classroom. Our intention is for the teachers to thrive (i.e., produce student learning gains, enjoy positive relationships with faculty and students, grow professionally), but being too attached to how those teachers reach that goal could restrict ideas, strategies, and out-of-the-box approaches that just might work. On the other hand, if someone has *low intention*, they might lack the drive and energy to take action and complete the tasks and steps needed to help the teachers reach their own goals. Worse, if an individual has *low intention* and *low attachment*, they likely would lack the motivation to pursue the outcome and would cling to the present circumstances, possibly afraid to let go of old ideas and approaches because "that's the way we always have done it." Therefore, the right mix—the sweet spot—is for a person to have *high intention* and *low attachment*, meaning they move assertively and persistently toward an outcome but are not fixed on a particular method or approach to get there. With this attitude, the supervisor would have the flexibility and responsiveness needed to continually adjust until finding ways to help teachers under their care become successful.

High Intention	High Attachment
Low Intention	Low Attachment

Figure 7.1. Intention and Attachment Matrix
Courtesy of author

LETTING GO AND NON-STRIVING IN EDUCATIONAL SUPERVISION

Applying the concept of letting go to supervision can take many forms. The first area might be releasing limiting ideas, thoughts, and beliefs around teaching and learning and coaching educators that are not serving you or those you supervise. While this can be different for individuals, perhaps you have limited beliefs about what teachers can accomplish at various levels of development. Maybe you have a limiting belief about your own practice, such as *I can only effectively coach a certain type of teacher*, or *I can only coach several teachers before my attention gets scattered*.

Understanding exactly where we may be holding onto limiting beliefs and views as a supervisor of teachers can be further explored by examining Sergiovanni and Starratt's (2007) work detailing four supervisory "types" or "images." Supervisor A is described as authoritarian, subscribing to a highly structured teaching and learning system with clear objectives, curriculum, assessment, and teaching methods. Supervisor B's focus is on relationships and working closely with teachers, with the concern on the "teaching system's insensitivity to teachers' needs" (p. 21). Supervisor C also values teacher relationships but believes that successful teaching and learning occur when teacher motivation is high, which results from being given autonomy and sharing values and responsibility. Finally, Supervisor D "relies much less on direct supervision," believing that external forces, such as community building, culture, norms, and relational trust result in effective teaching and academic success. Of course these images are caricatures or oversimplifications of supervisory approaches. More realistically, you might be a combination of these images, but knowing them can help us situate and clarify our educational supervision beliefs, views, and mindsets.

WHAT'S IN YOUR SUPERVISION BACKPACK?

Studying various supervision stances can help us decide what to let go: ideologies, beliefs, views, and practices that might no longer be suited for the current teaching field or education system. Views on teacher relationships, evaluation procedures and tools, delivery systems for feedback, time management and priorities . . . what might be holding you back from coaching teachers in a way that empowers them and enables them to grow professionally and enhance student learning? What needs to be "dropped"? Before proceeding, it might help to craft an *educational platform* (see Sergiovanni & Starratt, 2007, pp. 82–97). Such a platform features elements such as one's beliefs on the aim of education; views of knowledge and learning; images of the learner, curriculum, and teacher; and preferred pedagogy and school climate. Taking time to write an educational platform can flesh out the specific beliefs and thoughts (including self-limiting ones) we possess.

Freeing ourselves from limiting beliefs and practices can help us as supervisors live and work from the present moment and with more intention, care, and flexibility. There is a story of the Buddha when he would teach his disciples about the concept of letting go in the mind. Walking through the forest, he would have them hold a heavy branch then tell them to "let it go." They would instantly recognize the relief of releasing the weight when walking. In a similar vein, it might help for us as educational leaders to imagine we carry a *supervision backpack* full of ideas, beliefs, and practices. Examining what's in the backpack and what might be needed to be discarded serves as a metaphor for letting go. The backpack image in figure 7.2 can help you determine what you might need to throw out of your metaphorical backpack. To use this tool, on the left side, list your major supervision-related beliefs, views, and practices. On the right side, note the ones that might be holding you back or weighing you down and that you need to let go.

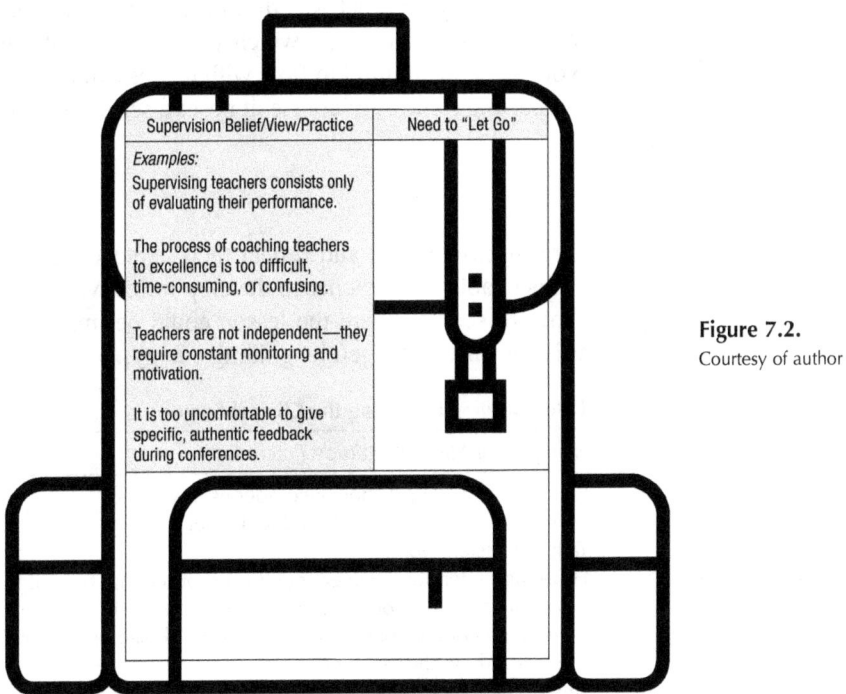

Figure 7.2.
Courtesy of author

CULTIVATING LETTING GO AND NON-STRIVING DURING THE CLINICAL SUPERVISION CYCLE

The following section addresses ways in which letting go and non-striving can inform the clinical stages.

Pre-Conference

You might have to let go of ingrained ideas, beliefs, or expectations regarding what "good teaching" *should* look like. Instead, embrace a beginner's mind and be open to different approaches and new possibilities. As much as possible based on their current development stage, allow the teacher to lead the conference and share the lesson. Go with the flow—unless you intuitively feel you need to add or step in. Sometimes *less is more* in the sense that the less you talk or advise, the more the teacher has space to articulate their teaching strategies and approach.

Classroom Observation

During the observation, remind yourself to let go of what you are supposed to observe during the lesson. Prior to observing, intentionally release expectations. If something doesn't align with what was discussed during the pre-conference, go with it by taking accurate notes, which you can share at the post-conference. Allow your senses and mind to flow with the lesson; release any resistance to what is occurring (unless, of course, it poses a serious physical threat to students).

Post-Conference

Allow the teacher space to discuss, share, and reflect their perspectives on how the teaching went. This enables the teacher to develop reflective thinking. Guide them gently toward seeing where the lesson could be improved with minimal effort or striving. Just add a gentle, guiding energy.

Table 7.1. Letting Go and Non-Striving Informing the Clinical Stages

Clinical Stage	Examples of Mindful Attitude Practices
Pre-Conference	Practice releasing preconceived notions of what an "effective" lesson plan should look like.
	Talk less, listen more.
Classroom Observation	Have high intention (give energy toward observing) but with low attachment (not fixed on any one outcome).
	Release preconceptions of what you "should" see or "expect" to see. Allow the teaching to unfold.
Post-Conference	Talk and advise less; allow more space for the teacher to articulate and reflect.
	Let go of limiting beliefs about the teacher or their capabilities. See the possibilities.

LETTING GO AND THE IMMEDIATE RESPONSE SKILLS

Noticing

Sometimes as supervisors, whether a principal working with a first-year teacher or a university supervisor working with teacher candidates, we really want to see something happen in the classroom, an amazing teachable moment come to light: intense student engagement, expert pacing, creative use of technology, a deep debate or discussion on a topic. We are looking *hard* for these moments; however, letting go means taking a breath and relaxing into the lesson. Be present as the teaching occurs and, like a mirror, take notes and collect data on what actually happens, not what we wish to happen or want to observe. This is easier said than done, but non-striving in this situation would mean recording only what is necessary for effective feedback and the growth of the teacher—no more, no less.

Ignoring

The response skill of ignoring is essentially letting go. As you observe a teacher, you may feel the need to write down every teachable moment, every word and action that transpires; but realistically, you will only have time to discuss so many moments during the follow-up conference. Besides, presenting too many teachable moments at one time will only confuse or overwhelm the teacher. Therefore, during an observation you will have to practice letting go of some of those moments. Take a breath and tell yourself to "let go" as you decide not to record a particular moment or, later, go through a list of teachable events and cross some off.

MINDFULNESS-BASED PRACTICES FOR LETTING GO

Breath Meditation

Returning to the practice of sitting in meditation each day, we can bring a gentle focus to the importance of letting go. As you experience the flow of breath, observe how there is a "let go" on the outward breath. If you try to hold onto the breath, it becomes nearly impossible and disrupts the natural movement of the breath. Without manipulation, experience your breathing, paying particular attention to how the breath leaves the nostrils and enters the environment. During the exhalation, you can sense or imagine various experiences leaving you, like bodily tension, stress, anxiety, or frustration.

Supervision Context

Try bringing this feeling of letting go into your supervisory role. When you feel tense, overwhelmed, or constricted in your awareness, you can turn to the breath as a reminder of the power of letting go. As the breath leaves the body, allow the idea, belief, emotion, or other mental block to release.

Four Foundations of Mindfulness Practice

Another way to cultivate a letting-go quality is to meditate using the Four Foundations of Mindfulness discussed earlier. Along with observing the breath, pay attention to various feelings and sensations in the body during sitting meditation. Experience how thoughts and sensations possess a transitory nature. Become aware of how our minds tend to cling to pleasant thoughts or certain experiences and push away others.

Supervision Context

As you work with teachers, have a subtle awareness of the transitory nature of your thoughts, feelings, and experience in general. Remind yourself that in education and supervision, things have a rhythm, a flow, and in time will change. Try to work with this energy rather than resist and hold onto experiences, situations, or approaches that may need to be let go.

Letting Go Meditation

This meditation method is adapted from mindfulness teacher Jack Kornfield. Sit comfortably with eyes closed and bring a kind of awareness to your breath. Allow yourself a few minutes to come to the present moment. Bring to your awareness any story, situation, feeling, or reaction that needs to be let go (e.g., anger, jealousy, resentment, worry). Allow yourself to feel that emotion within the space of compassionate awareness. Ask yourself questions such as *Do I have to continue to replay this story? Do I have to hold on to these losses, these feelings? Is it time to let this go?* Feel what it might feel like to let go. You can gently follow this with the mantra "Let go, let go" as you watch the breath go out. You can imagine any emotions or tension leaving you like water draining from a tub. Sit easily in this space. Take a moment and then slowly open your eyes.

Supervision Context

The Letting Go Meditation can be woven into your weekly sitting meditation. You might feel the need to engage in the Letting Go meditation more frequently if you experience difficulty releasing an emotion or circumstance that is limiting your supervision abilities.

Experiencing Emotions as a Form of Letting Go

This exercise is best done when experiencing an emotion, perhaps one that is noticeable but not too intense. Take a sitting meditation position on the floor or relaxed in a chair. Close your eyes and tune into your body. Allow yourself to feel the emotion. Imagine witnessing it as if it were an energy or a storm passing by. Notice the transitory nature of the emotion, how it comes and begins to go. Breathe into the emotion, seeing if you can let it go.

Supervision Context

Become more aware of your emotions and feelings during supervision. When beginning to feel frustrated, annoyed, excited, or even angry, notice the emotion and practice observing or witnessing it as a fluid energy.

EXAMPLE OF LETTING GO AND NON-STRIVING IN SUPERVISION

Pre-Conference

Prior to meeting with a teacher, Principal Warren sat quietly reflecting on the ideas and beliefs she held about working with this educator. She listed a few beliefs, such as *I think this teacher should be further along in her development by year two. Her classroom management is not where it needs to be exactly. Her planning for pacing and assessment is still off—other teachers at this stage have this down.* Closing her eyes, she focused gently on her breath then mentally repeated "let it go" as she imagined these preconceptions floating away. Feeling more open and spacious, she conferenced with the teacher, Mrs. Stinson, listening deeply to her description of the upcoming lesson, taking note of exact plans on management and assessment but reserving judgment or appearing impatient. Principal Warren noticed that Mrs. Stinson had reflected and presented a slightly more sophisticated approach to grouping students and organizing materials, which could help with management of the lesson. When Mrs. Stinson finished talking, Warren suggested a few other strategies.

Classroom Observation

While watching the teacher's lesson, Warren listed various teachable moments and recorded data. Rather than impose her views on the teaching experience, Warren flowed with the lesson, being more open to how it unfolded, how Mrs. Stinson introduced the topic, and how the students responded to instruction. Though Warren wrote down 12 different teachable moments that could be discussed, she took a breath and crossed out (and let go) seven of those moments, deciding to focus on the remaining moments that centered on management and assessment.

Post-Conference

After the observation, Warren met with Mrs. Stinson, asking her guiding questions, including "How did you think the lesson went?" and "Do you think students achieved the learning outcomes? How do you know?" Warren skillfully directed the conversation to a few teachable moments, such as when classroom management improved (having students put away materials) but was still lacking (when Mrs. Stinson used several attention grabbers, the students did not respond and kept talking). She listened mindfully and caringly to Mrs. Stinson, and as the conversation went deeper and the teacher demonstrated critical reflective thinking on her pedagogy, Warren flowed with the discussion, deciding to let go of a few other teachable moments in her observation notes. She decided she could share those insights later, in writing.

WHAT'S NEXT?

In chapter 8 you will learn how acceptance and non-judgment can empower supervision.

Chapter Eight

Acceptance and Non-Judgment in Supervision

Acceptance and non-judgment are essential components of mindfulness practice, providing a more compassionate and accepting approach to themselves, others, and their surroundings. Though not commonly related with supervision, these qualities can inform supervision work in new ways. Acceptance, in the context of mindfulness practice, means seeing things as they are, as they unfold in the present moment. Eventually, we must come to terms with a situation as it is—particularly if we want to change it. As Lindsay and colleagues (2018) have described it while studying how mindfulness reduces stress, in contrast to avoidance or trying to change negative stimuli, "Acceptance is an attitude of receptivity and equanimity toward all momentary experiences that allows even stressful stimuli to arise and pass without reactivity" (p. 63). Practicing acceptance involves experiencing thoughts, emotions, and bodily sensations—both pleasant and unpleasant—without judgment. Instead, we approach these experiences with a sense of openness and curiosity.

Nevertheless, acceptance often carries a negative connotation. When we hear the word "acceptance," it is often misconstrued to mean that we must remain passive, resigning ourselves to put up with or be satisfied with current conditions. This is not at all the meaning of mindful acceptance. Rather, acceptance with mindful awareness allows us to see things clearly, as they are, without mentally constructed bias or barriers. From this place, we are in the best position to effect change. We come to terms with what is happening in the present, and with mental clarity, presence, and intentionality, we do what is necessary to improve the situation (if that is possible).

During meditation practice, acceptance helps avoid fighting against what arises. For example, we don't impose our ideas on the meditative experience or force certain thoughts. Instead, acceptance allows the meditator to be present with what arises in the mind or body, simply experiencing and reflecting *what is*. We cultivate the ability to be receptive, to openly receive whatever thought, image, or sensation comes. Cultivating acceptance in meditation practice—being more accepting with ourselves—can help individuals feel more compassionate with themselves and their environment.

Furthermore, acceptance can reduce the stress and anxiety that come with trying to change or control experiences. Acceptance and commitment therapy (ACT), in which acceptance serves as a major component, has been shown to reduce symptoms of anxiety and depression (Hayes et al., 2006). Researchers (Lindsay et al., 2018) emphasized the role of acceptance within mindfulness-based interventions, noting that "acceptance is a critical component of mindfulness training for reducing biological stress reactivity; without acceptance training, mindfulness stress buffering effects are diminished or eliminated" (p. 70).

Another essential component in mindfulness training, non-judgment involves observing experience in the present moment without evaluating or analyzing whether it's good or bad, right or wrong. While sounding nearly impossible, non-judgment is the ability to directly experience the moment without bias. We learn to become aware of the judging quality of the mind (Kabat-Zinn, 1990) and let go of preconceptions. Non-judgment means superseding the mind's tendency to evaluate and label. Mindful non-judgment relates closely to acceptance, approaching experiences with openness and curiosity, and beginner's mind. Mindfulness teachers believe that enhancing the quality of non-judgment can promote greater self-awareness and understanding and increase connection with others.

During meditation practice, non-judgment teaches us to become a more impartial witness and grow aware of the mind's constant labeling. For example, while observing your breath, you may notice thoughts such as *This is boring. Is this working?* or *I'm having too many thoughts.* At this moment, you become aware that these are simply judgments and, without reacting or entertaining them, allow the thoughts to pass. Regular mindfulness meditation causes us to recognize how the mind constantly categorizes experiences—good, bad, or neutral—and locks us into unconscious, often-limiting patterns. This constant judging within the mind can also be stressful and interfere with experiencing any peace.

ACCEPTANCE AND NON-JUDGMENT IN EDUCATIONAL SUPERVISION

Within the context of a mindfulness-based supervision approach, acceptance and non-judgment have the potential to enhance the process in various ways—for example, accepting that a teacher under your supervision is not developing at the expected rate, or that a mentor teacher and teacher candidate are not bonding or the relationship is not fostering growth.

Acceptance that as a supervisor, you are human and can only provide a certain level of support or be available at certain times of the day due to your pressing responsibilities as a superintendent, principal, or university supervisor. Withholding judgment when listening to a lesson plan for an upcoming observation (waiting to the appropriate time to evaluate and respond) or practicing open awareness rather than labeling every minute of an observation as it happens.

As educational supervisors, we must be mindful that we are working within a complex area—dealing with relationships, power dynamics, performance evaluations, and other factors to become highly critical or judgmental. Mindfulness attitudes of acceptance and non-judgment can allow us to maintain perspective and come to terms with what we can change, what we cannot, and the optimal times to take action.

CULTIVATING ACCEPTANCE AND NON-JUDGMENT DURING THE CLINICAL SUPERVISION CYCLE

Pre-Conference

When meeting with teachers to discuss their lesson plans, acceptance does not mean passively receiving whatever is presented. Mindful acceptance positions supervisors to listen openly and deeply, allowing the situation to transpire as it is, without overreacting. We practice patience and provide room for a teacher, including a struggling one, to think through their teaching and explain their rationale in areas of assessment, teaching strategies, selection of materials, technology usage, and other components. We strive to be mindfully aware of the judging quality of our minds, the instinct to quickly dismiss ideas or question what is said. With this attitude, we wait until the teacher has fully articulated their pedagogical approach; then, from a place of centeredness and open awareness, we begin to ask questions and make suggestions. Examples of mindful practices during clinical supervision are provided in table 8.1.

Classroom Observation

Acceptance and non-judgment might be most difficult to practice when observing teachers. Often, based on our own preconceptions and past experience as teachers, we snap to judgment when watching others teach in the

Table 8.1. Acceptance and Non-Judgment During the Clinical Supervision Cycle

Clinical Stage	Examples of Mindful Attitude Practices
Pre-Conference	Listen openly to the teacher's articulation of the upcoming observation plan.
	Withhold the mind's judging quality, allow the teacher to fully explain and present their lesson plans.
Classroom Observation	Be present with the observation, not engaging in the judging of each teaching technique, method, or learning activity.
Post-Conference	Withhold the instinct to judge or evaluate each comment provided by the teacher as they describe their observed lesson. Remain receptive and open until the proper time to provide specific feedback and support.

classroom. We quickly label pedagogical practices and methods as "good" or "bad," as "effective" or "noneffective." As supervisors, we may struggle against the moment if the teaching does not appear to be going well (e.g., students talking over the teacher's direction, lack of student engagement). However, these mindful attitudes can help us better coach educators by providing us with a lens of open receptivity, acting with less reactivity and withholding judgment until we have at least given the teacher a chance to explain their rationale and the situation. For example, what might appear as a negative relationship between teacher and student or poor classroom management could be the result of a student not having slept the night before due to a family conflict or the death of a loved one. Without mindful acceptance, non-judgment, and patience, a supervisor may never take the time to explore the situation and simply rely on observational data.

Post-Conference

Again, bringing the attitudes of acceptance and non-judgment does not mean that, as educational supervisors, we don't provide pointed feedback, but rather that we don't rush to judgment or bring forth hasty opinions when debriefing a teacher over their lesson. Mindfulness positions us to be fully present with a teacher as they explain how they think their lesson went—without interruption or mentally labeling each and every word. Then, when the time is right, we compassionately provide the necessary feedback and direction based on that teacher's developmental level.

Teachable Moments

Practicing mindful acceptance and non-judgment within the context of noticing and recording teachable moments can be extremely challenging. Our minds naturally want to categorize and label every moment as positive, negative, or neutral. Perhaps it might help to simply list all the teachable moments you recognize during an observation, withholding any judgment. Then later, after the lesson is finished, sit quietly and go back over the list, contemplating specific moments and what impact each had on the teaching and student learning.

MINDFULNESS-BASED STRATEGIES TO CULTIVATE ACCEPTANCE AND NON-JUDGMENT

Acknowledging as a Form of Acceptance

One technique to cultivate mindful acceptance during meditation practice, as well as in your supervision work, is to acknowledge whatever is happening. For instance, when sitting to meditate, you notice many thoughts racing through your mind. Rather than resist this experience (nonacceptance), try *acknowledging* it. As thoughts occur, simply say to yourself, "Okay, I am having lots of thoughts," or "My mind is very busy."

Supervision Context

Try acknowledging whatever happens during supervision without fighting it or adding extra stress to the situation. For example, you are coaching a struggling beginning teacher who is not making the expected progress. Rather than become upset, gently acknowledge the situation ("This teacher is not progressing") and acknowledge your feelings about the situation ("This situation is upsetting me"). With this awareness, you can work to move past judgment and the associated stress to being present with what is going on and respond in a manner that is best for everyone involved.

Cultivating Acceptance and Non-Judgment During Meditation

When practicing sitting meditation (which this book has hopefully convinced you to try), gently bring the attitudes of acceptance and non-judgment to your experience. As thoughts arise (and they naturally will), observe them as an impartial witness, without reacting or labeling them. Watch them pass by like clouds in the sky. Bring a sense of whatever happens—whether the meditation is cognitively busy, restless, pleasant or not, accept the experience.

Supervision Context

After sitting in meditation, while working in your educational leadership role, recall these attitudes of acceptance and non-judgment when dealing with various circumstances, such as listening to a teacher describe a pedagogical problem, watching a lesson, or seeing students respond to learning in various ways. Bring that impartial witness to the thoughts and notions that surface.

Keep a Non-Judgment Journal

Similar to a gratitude journal, we can regularly record our experiences with judging. In your journal, list judgments you made during the day, experiences, people, situations, objects you have classified. Also record the emotions that accompanied these judgments. Over time, you may start to recognize patterns—circumstances and times during supervision when you tend to be overly critical or evaluative. With this awareness, you can reflect on how you prefer to perceive these situations.

Supervision Context

You can link the journaling activity to specific areas of supervision to identify when you are most judgmental. For example, divide your journal entries into the clinical stages (pre-conference, observation, etc.) and list judgments you made during these stages. Periodically revisit these entries to recognize where changes can be made.

WHAT'S NEXT?

In chapter 9 you will entertain how gratitude and generosity can benefit supervision.

Chapter Nine

Gratitude and Generosity (Yes, in Supervision)

Gratitude has been described as both a trait and an emotional state (Jans-Beken et al., 2020). Feeling gratitude is similar to feeling a sense of appreciation. The American Psychological Association (n.d.) defines gratitude as a sense of happiness and thankfulness in response to something good that has happened or receiving a tangible gift. Gratitude is a prosocial behavior that is very much linked to our survival as a species. Expressing gratitude can serve as a way to communicate reciprocal interaction and prevent a person from being seen as a "freeloader," which could result in social punishment—for instance, being excommunicated from a group (de Qurvain et al., 2004). Therefore, gratitude is an emotion that can maintain social connections and ensure a person's social standing, signaling to others that they are a fair partner.

Feeling gratitude comes in two stages (Emmons & McCullough, 2003). The first is a general acknowledgment of goodness in life, that life has elements that make it worth living. The second stage involves understanding that sources of this goodness are external (e.g., a creator, people, animals, nature). The good news is that since gratitude is a trait, it can be strengthened through various practices and daily habits (McCullough et al., 2002). The cultivation of gratitude has been a focus in the field of positive psychology, which studies how to increase optimism, hope, resiliency, and well-being. For example, gratitude is a key component in Seligman's PERMA Model (2011), which posits that five components, including positive emotions, relationships, and meaning, contribute to well-being and a happy life. There has been an increased interest in studying gratitude empirically. Studies suggest that the practice of gratitude improves physical, emotional, and psychological well-being; increases resilience to trauma; and enhances social relationships (Fox et. al., 2015; Jans-Beken et al., 2020; Wood et al., 2010). Research shows that people who maintain weekly gratitude journals tend to exercise regularly, have fewer physical health problems, and feel generally more optimistic (Jans-Beken et al., 2020). Just having daily discussions of gratitude can cause higher levels of energy, alertness, enthusiasm, and better sleep. Individuals who are grateful are also more likely to recognize when others are helpful and reciprocate.

Focusing on gratitude reverses the brain's hardwiring to detect potentially negative situations as a means of defense and survival. Gratitude practices, completed regularly, even as little as a few times per week, can counteract our negativity bias, creating a wedge in the brain between negative feelings and prosocial positive feelings (Huberman, 2021). While common gratitude activities such as keeping a gratitude journal or talking about what one is thankful for can have positive effects, "receiving gratitude" appears to be even more powerful. For example, reading a gratitude letter you received from someone would have more positive impact than simply writing one yourself. Researchers found that having people watch documentaries of Holocaust survivors receiving food and clothing by those offering shelter and then imagine themselves as those survivors and what it would feel like to receive those gifts experienced higher degrees of neurological impact (Fox et al., 2015).

Mindfulness and gratitude are complementary and intertwined. Practicing present-moment awareness, we can better recognize, and thus appreciate, the people, material possessions, circumstances, and small things in our lives. A mindful attitude toward gratitude focuses mindfulness on the cultivation of positive feelings and well-being.

Like gratitude, generosity is a prosocial behavior deeply ingrained into our evolutionary survival as a species. The term "generosity" is generally defined as helping or cooperative behavior (Allen, 2018). While humans might be considered selfish, studies show that generosity is more than a cultural construct and that the instinct for generous behavior has deep, evolutionary roots. A growing body of evidence suggests that we are hardwired to be generous. For example, several studies found that when people help others, their brain activity mirrors those associated with parental caregiving (Swain et al., 2012). During the act of giving, the same neural circuits are activated as when we eat or have sexual intercourse. When we do something that feels good, we are likely programmed to do it again; these feel-good behaviors are fundamentally part of our survival.

As with practicing gratitude, being generous is good medicine. Growing evidence suggests that acts of generosity can reduce psychological problems and improve subjective well-being. For example, a meta-analysis of 37 studies published between 1968 and 1994 showed that 70 percent of individuals who volunteered their time reported a greater quality of life than those who did not, even after controlling for socioeconomics or health (Wheeler et al., 1998). Specifically, there seems to be a link between being generous and being happy. While we might think focusing on yourself produces happiness, studies show just the opposite. Being generous makes you happier.

According to Kabat-Zinn, an attitude of generosity provides a solid foundation for the practice of mindfulness. When practicing mindfulness, such as sitting meditation, you can give yourself gifts such as self-acceptance or grace. You can give yourself time to just be, to have no agenda. We can extend this mindful attitude of generosity toward others, with no expectation of gain or return, simply enjoying the act of giving. Furthermore, we can be mindful of any resistance to giving, intentionally gifting more in small increments.

GRATITUDE AND GENEROSITY IN EDUCATIONAL SUPERVISION

At first glance, cultivating mindful attitudes of gratitude and generosity might seem out of place within supervision. However, practicing these attitudes can significantly impact your relationships with teachers, ability to coach and provide feedback, and empower educators. If anything, as research shows, being thankful and giving (in this case, as part of your work) is just plain for good for you. How can you express mindful gratitude as an education leader? On one level, you can bring this attitude into your personal mindfulness practice (specific methods to be described later in the chapter). Appreciate the chance to sit quietly, to take a mindful walk, to pause during the busy school day and just be with the breath. Express gratitude for being in a profession where you can have a profound impact on others, including young people and those who work directly for hours a day. While, as supervisors, we often get caught up worrying or frustrated with teachers struggling to perform in the classroom, we can be grateful for those who are progressing and skillful teachers, who have remained in the field despite the many challenges. Generosity can manifest in supervision in various ways as well: being generous in providing encouragement to teachers and others under our direction, being generous with our time, and being generous with feedback. We can also be generous with ourselves as part of a mindfulness practice, giving ourselves time, space, and "permission," to de-stress, center, and connect.

CULTIVATING GRATITUDE AND GENEROSITY DURING THE CLINICAL SUPERVISION CYCLE

Pre-Conference

Being grateful during the pre-conference stage could look like just thanking the teacher for their time, input, and attention. Perhaps before meeting, you could take a mindful moment to reflect on the opportunities to work closely with educators and effect positive change. If time permits, you could list the positives of working with a particular teacher. Generosity could take the form of providing lots of encouragement and a generous amount of guidance (if developmentally appropriate) during the planning phase.

Classroom Observation

When watching a teacher in action, supervisors can be grateful for the opportunity to experience a professional expressing and developing their craft. We have been invited into *someone else's workspace*, and that in itself is a reason to be thankful. Supervisors can be generous when collecting evidence of effective teaching, maybe gathering more than what is needed at the time, but having choices later to narrow it down. We can also cultivate a mindful generosity by spending time searching for powerful teachable moments in the class, when learning comes alive.

Post-Conference

During this stage of the clinical cycle, supervisors can be grateful for a chance to meet again with a teacher and take part in their professional growth. We can provide *lots* of encouragement and generous amounts of constructive feedback that encourages deeper reflection and pedagogical progression.

Examples of mindful attitude practices during the clinical supervision cycle are provided in table 9.1.

Table 9.1. Gratitude and Generosity During the Clinical Supervision Cycle

Clinical Stage	Examples of Mindful Attitude Practices
Pre-Conference	Reflect on what you are grateful for (e.g., regarding the teacher, your role as supervisor) *prior* to the conference.
	Be generous in your feedback, encouragement, and (if possible) time.
Classroom Observation	Practice gratitude for the opportunity to watch a teacher practice their craft and help them grow professionally.
	Be generous in collecting data and evidence of teaching/learning (e.g., take copious notes, use a variety of evidence).
Post-Conference	Be thankful for the chance to help a teacher learn to reflect on their craft.
	Be generous in providing meaningful feedback, support, and direction.

MINDFULNESS-BASED STRATEGIES TO CULTIVATE GRATITUDE AND GENEROSITY

Ask "Gratitude" Questions

A simple gratitude practice is to intentionally ask questions that cause us to reflect on what we have versus what is lacking. Following a morning meditation session or right before going to sleep at night, ask yourself questions such as W*hat am I thankful for* or *What can I be thankful for? What beautiful things exist around me? What have I received? Who can I really appreciate? Who has helped me in my life?* Don't force answers. Just ask the questions from a space of openness and awareness.

Supervision Context

Educational leaders can bring such questions into their work. For example, prior to the school day, ask, *What can I be grateful for regarding my work and individuals I work with?* Walking down the school hallway, supervisors can ponder, *What positive things are happening on campus? How are adults and students using their abilities, talents, and creativity to create change?* Consider where you can insert gratitude questions into your work schedule.

Keeping a Gratitude Journal

One of the most highly recommended strategies to cultivate gratitude is to keep a journal. The idea is to establish a daily routine where you journal about events, people, and situations you are grateful for. Upon waking, maybe while sipping morning coffee or tea, you might journal. While there is no one way to keep a gratitude journal, there are some recommendations. One strategy is to write five things for which you are grateful (the act of writing it down is suggested to be more powerful than just mentally repeating it). While journaling about a good event, experience, person, or thing, try to enjoy the positive emotions that accompany it. Be specific, and provide as much detail as possible. Savor surprises and see the good things as "gifts" not to be taken for granted. Also, it's important to write regularly (Greater Good Science Center, 2023).

Supervision Context

Keeping a gratitude journal can be done prior to heading to work. However, you might be able to incorporate brief journaling during the school day. For example, a principal sitting in the office, though incredibly busy, could take two minutes to list things they are grateful for and savor the emotions that accompany it. A university supervisor could journal while waiting for a teacher candidate to arrive at a scheduled conference. It's a matter of creatively working journaling into one's supervisory tasks.

Gratitude Meditation

A more formal method of cultivating gratitude is to practice a sitting meditation centered on gratefulness. This meditation, drawn from the work of mindfulness teacher Jack Kornfield, could be done at the end of your regular breath meditation or serve as its own meditation. Begin by sitting comfortably with the eyes closed. Allow your body to relax and breathing to be natural. Acknowledge everything that has supported your life.

> *With gratitude, I recall all the people, animals, elements of earth (water, air, etc.) that support my life every day.*
> *With gratitude, I remember all the generations of ancestors that have come before me.*
> *I am grateful for the well-being and safety I have received.*
> *I express gratitude for the family and friends I have been given.*
> *I offer gratitude for the community I enjoy.*
> *I am grateful for the teachings, lessons, and knowledge I have received.*
> *I offer gratitude for the life I have been given.*

Return gently to the breath. Be aware of how the body feels, particularly in the heart area. When ready, slowly open your eyes.

Supervision Context

Along with practicing this gratitude meditation at home, look for ways to engage in "mini" meditations throughout the school day. Perhaps take a minute or two in your office to focus on the breath and silently repeat a few of the gratitude phrases listed above.

Practicing Generosity

One of the simplest ways to practice generosity is a habit that had been recommended by mindfulness teachers Joseph Goldstein and Jack Kornfield. Anytime you have a thought to be generous or to give something, and you are in a position to do it, then do it. For example, you are cooking some food and have the thought to make some for your neighbor or co-worker (and are in a position to buy and make a little extra)—do it. If you have the thought to pay someone a compliment, do it. Build the generosity habit. In time, generous behavior will become an automatic response.

Supervision Context

Be mindful of when you have a thought to do something generous when working in your supervision role. Maybe it's the thought to visit a teacher in their classroom and thank them for how hard they work. It could be the thought to spend more time meeting with a beginning teacher who needs more support and encouragement.

Giving Creatively

While giving money might be most associated with generosity, there are many ways to give that are not material in nature. Be creative in your mindset and open to various forms of giving. You can offer a smile or a friendly greeting. If someone is anxious or fearful, we can give in the form of providing a grounded, calm presence. We can also give our time and energy to helping someone or to a cause. Other ways to give that do not involve finances include giving undivided attention, knowledge, advice, and wisdom.

Supervision Context

Look for nonmaterial ways to give in your supervision role. For example, can you provide compassion, attention, or a grounded presence to a teacher in need? Might a teacher need you to give more support in their classroom? Maybe give your time by co-teaching a lesson or collecting additional data and sharing more feedback?

EXAMPLE OF GRATITUDE AND GENEROSITY INFORMING THE CLINICAL CYCLE

Pre-Conference

While sipping her morning coffee, well before she steps foot on campus, Principal Warren takes a few minutes to reflect on what she is grateful for, noting it in her journal. She relives the emotions of being able to support and connect with teachers and provide an inclusive, nourishing environment for students. (Remember, this is not the time to ruminate on the challenges of the job, e.g., unreasonable state mandates, testing pressures, angry parents; there will be plenty of time for that later.) While waiting for Mrs. Stinson to arrive at her office for the pre-conference, Warren pauses, observes her breath for a few minutes, then silently asks herself a few gratitude questions, such as *What is it that I enjoy about working with this teacher? What do I appreciate (or can be appreciative) about her?*

When Mrs. Stinson walks in, Warren has the thought to offer a bottle of water, so she follows through. The small act of kindness, along with a smile, seems to put Stinson more at ease. Although the pre-conference is scheduled for 20 minutes, Principal Warren intentionally gives a few extra minutes to provide guidance and encouragement.

Classroom Observation

Before observing Mrs. Stinson, Warren briefly expresses gratitude for being able to visit the classroom and watch the educator and students in action. When collecting data, Warren takes generous notes, recording not only concerns or areas of enhancement but also many examples of positive, teachable moments.

Post-Conference

Principal Warren greets Mrs. Stinson warmly, thanking her for the opportunity to observe her teach and collaborate on her professional growth. Within the time limits, Warren provides the teacher with appropriate space to accurately describe and reflect on the lesson and the student learning, without interruption. As much as possible, Warren openly shares her observations, outlining several teachable moments garnered from the lesson. Like during the pre-conference, Warren extends the conference a few minutes to provide direction and encouragement.

WHAT'S NEXT?

In the concluding chapter we explore how mindfulness can support inclusive school leadership.

Chapter Ten

Mindfulness-Informed Educational Leadership

Moving Toward a More Inclusive Approach to Supervision

The purpose of this book is to provide educational leaders with mindfulness-based tools and strategies to inform supervision practice. However, the reason for this book is to push the paradigm of how teachers are coached and supervised, to expand the theoretical lens, and broaden our conception of school leadership. Approaching supervision with mindfulness attitudes of presence, beginner's mind, acceptance, non-judgment, and other qualities can truly be transformative. For example, conferencing with a teacher is no longer just a meeting but also becomes a space for deeper listening, compassionate presence, flow, rhythmic energy, and responsiveness. An observation morphs into an experience of immersion, curiosity, awareness, and enjoyment. Through mindfulness, both supervisor and supervisee can experience positive change.

While this book has focused on mindfulness methods assisting the individual school leader, this final chapter will serve to enlarge that scope, to move from individual transformation to campus-wide change, with the emphasis on inclusiveness. The basis of this chapter originates from several edited book chapters by the author and a colleague (Haberlin & Mette, 2023; Haberlin, 2023) aimed at how mindfulness practices can inform culturally responsive, inclusive, and equitable supervision. Why the need for a more inclusive, mindfulness-informed supervision?

The truth is that we have a long way to go make our educational systems and practices inclusive, equitable, and effective. In the past 50 years, closing racial achievement (also known as the opportunity gap) in US public schools remains an issue. (Khalifa et al., 2016; Khalifa, 2011, 2020; Payne, 2008). Consider the following: Students in historically repressed groups remain marginalized, with academic performance between highest and lowest socio-economic groups showing little change (Khalifa et al., 2016).

In particular, achievement gaps between White and Black students have experienced "little change over the last two decades" (Hanushek et al., 2019; pp. 4–5). Schools are expected to become even more culturally and racially diverse while about 80 percent of the teaching workforce still remains White.

What can we do to meet these challenges? Where can we leverage educational structures and practices? As Mette and colleagues (2020) argue, one of the most practical and straightforward approaches to support a more inclusive, culturally responsive education model is through culturally responsive instructional supervision. Educational leaders, such as principals, hold power over highly influential aspects of teaching and learning, including policies, curriculum, and allocation of resources. Their decision-making in such matters is guided by their values, beliefs, past experiences, worldview, and possible bias—what has been deemed one's *critical consciousness* (Brown, 2004; Dantley, 2005a; Gay & Kirkland, 2003; McKenzie et al., 2008). Therefore, part of creating sustainable change is encouraging school leaders to move beyond thinking, reading, and discussing culturally responsive-related topics and engage in deep, self-reflective meditation that gets at the level of consciousness. School leaders need concrete methods for engaging in what Khalifa (2020) calls *critical self-reflection*, or critically and honestly looking inward at one's own values, beliefs, and life experiences.

The mindfulness attitudinal qualities featured in this book can assist with raising awareness to create a more inclusive form of supervision. By becoming more aware of ourselves, we can also grow in our awareness of others and how our thoughts, emotions, and actions impact our work. Just our *presence* alone can make someone feel included or not. Approaching supervision with a *beginner's mind* enables us to avoid bringing past experiences and bias into the present situation. *Patience* and *trust* provide a foundation to work with diverse individuals and groups. Mindfully *letting go* and *non-judgment* and *acceptance* again buffer supervisors against discriminatory practices. Finally, *gratitude* and *generosity* are the fuel to build positive connections with others, regardless of their background, ethnicity, or race. Taken together, these mindfulness attitudes position us to be more conscious and reflective of our values and beliefs as they come to teaching, learning, and life in general.

EMBODIED MINDFULNESS AS A TOOL FOR CRITICAL SELF-REFLECTION

However, to fully appreciate how mindfulness can assist school leaders in critical self-reflection, it's necessary to see how bias and racism can live in the body. For the purposes of this chapter, racism (along with other forms of discrimination) can be defined as malice against a person or group based on their race or ethnicity (Clark et al., 1999). Experiencing racism can have major physical and physiological impacts, passing from one generation to the next. The body, for example, lives in a constant state of stress or vigilance. Empirically, these effects can be found in differences in health among, for instance, Black males who accumulate stress through seemly subtle forms of racism or microaggressions (Watson, 2019).

Buddhism and other Eastern traditions have long believed that the body carries its own form of wisdom. Neuroscience now supports this notion, describing a mind-body system that is closely intertwined. This unique form of knowledge can often be felt as an expansion or constriction in the body, comfort or unpleasantness. As explored in the chapter on intuition, the body receives signals, or nudges. Advances in neuroscience show that our bodily structures are activated when we experience love, anger, fear, and other emotions.

THE BODY AND BIAS

Implicit bias surfaces as unconscious stereotypes and judgments about groups of people that impact our daily interactions, work lives, and communities (Blackwell, 2019). Our brains create schemas, or mental shortcuts, placing people, places, and objects into categories to make sense of our complex worlds (Fiske & Taylor, 1991). However, schemas can become highly problematic when we start assigning them to groups based on race, gender, ethnicity, and other differences. Without awareness, implicit bias can trigger our stress response, hijacking the brain's prefrontal cortex and activating the amygdala and overriding our ability to rationalize. Through embodied practices such as mindfulness, we can become more aware of implicit bias and related reactions and learn to disrupt these patterns. We can learn to settle our bodies and work and strengthen our "somatic muscle" by engaging in exercises that foster self-reflection and unearth the negative stress response in connection with race and other differences. For example, Blackwell (2019) suggests the following:

Recognize implicit bias by engaging in an honest assessment of your past and present experiences. Meditate on the people, situations, and places that make you feel uncomfortable or have a stress response. What might be the reason?

Feel what occurs in your body when you think about bias or schemas you might have created. Do you feel tightness in the chest, the stomach, the back of the shoulders and/or neck? Where does the discomfort reside? What happens to your breathing—does it become shallow or rapid?

Intentionally place yourself in situations and acknowledge what happens in your body. Purposely join groups or attend events with people of different sociocultural backgrounds and identities to increase awareness of your bodily responses.

THE INNER WORK OF CULTURALLY RESPONSIVE SUPERVISION

Mindfulness continues to be explored as a social justice tool and as a means to inquire how we might marginalize or minoritize others at a physiological level (see Magee, 2019; Owens, 2020). Cultivating present-moment, nonjudgmental awareness can help us examine unconscious, deeply rooted bias and prejudice. Likewise, embodied mindfulness involves the work of continually returning home to the body with present-moment awareness, tuning into feelings, sensations, and tensions (Owens, 2020). Magee (2019) in her work, which she refers to as *the inner work of racial justice*, sees mindfulness as a method that provides a gap between unconscious, negative cycles that reinforce separateness bias. Through regular practice, we gain a type of body insight. She writes:

> When anger arises suddenly, for example, we may find ourselves reacting in kind. Yet if we can notice the sensations that accompany anger and examine them, we may be able to learn something. We can slow down the reactive habit long enough to see what there is to see about our habits, our conditionings, our patterns of emotional. And we can choose a better way to respond. (p. 36)

For school leaders, this mindfulness gap and body insight can be of tremendous value, providing a contemplative structure to engage in the kind of critical reflection (Khalifa 2018, 2020) necessary to transform schools into truly inclusive environments. *Therefore, educational leaders, including superintendents, principals, teacher leaders, and university-based supervisors, could benefit by experimenting with various mindfulness meditation methods to become more aware their body's sensations and responses as they relate to culturally responsive supervision.* The following sections outline different embodied mindfulness exercises and practices within the context of inclusive supervision.

Body Scan

Revisit this mindfulness meditation method, described earlier in this book, as foundational for subsequent exercises. A complete description of the body scan can be found in chapter 5.

Mindfulness of Intentions Around Racial Justice Work

Based on Magee's 2019 work, this exercise employs mindfulness to perceive any discomfort caused by racism and any bias that might have resulted. Begin by sitting comfortably and focusing on the breath. Bring up the notion of racial justice and just allow whatever comes to mind; feel what happens in the body. Next, ask yourself: *Where am I seeing racism up close? How am I living notions tied to my own "race"?* Don't force answers; just allow anything to come up. Be mindful of what happens in your body. Then ask yourself: *What racial slurs am I using or hearing in my interactions with others? What stereotypes am I noticing about Black women or men? Asians? Latinos? Mexicans? Filipinos? Puerto Ricans?* Contemplate ideas or beliefs you might have picked up about race from your family or neighborhood. How do these ideas shade or influence information you pick up now from media? Continue to pay attention to bodily sensations. Notice any tightness or unpleasant feelings and where they occur. Further investigate by inquiring, *How might my notions of race, including those I picked up from family and my upbringing, be influencing, shaping, or affecting my work as a school leader? How are these unconscious beliefs and ideas driving or influencing my decisions on school policy, use of resources, school discipline, teacher recruitment, and other factors?*

Finally, simply sit with this experience and be present with "any pain or distress that remains" (Magee, 2019, p. 101).

Mindfulness of Community Exercise

This mindfulness exercise, also adapted from Magee (2019), can help educational leaders become more attuned to the nuances of their school communities. Start in a comfortable sitting position, close the eyes, and take a few deep breaths. Relax and observe the natural rhythm of the breath. Do a very brief body scan of the body, beginning with the feet and moving to the head. Visualize the neighborhood or community surrounding one of your earliest homes. *Whom do you picture? Who were the people there? What was the majority race? What race(s) did the service and work? Who were the leaders? What did it feel like to be in that community? Did you feel like you belonged? Did you feel like an outsider?* Allow yourself time to feel the reactions or sensations in the physical body.

Now consider: *How were the boundaries of the community formed (legal, social, cultural, or otherwise) that determined who was accepted and who was not? What do you know about that? How does it feel to reflect on this aspect of the community?* Again, just allow any thoughts, feelings, or physical sensations to arise and then sit with them. Allow them to dissolve. As the meditation comes to an end, reflect on *how others suffered from feeling apart, excluded, or marginalized*, and vow to bring compassion into your work.

The RAIN Method

RAIN, which stands for recognize, accept, investigate, and non-identify, is a mindfulness-based process that has been applied to examining racism within ourselves (see Magee, 2019). RAIN is essentially taking time in life to pause and deeply experience what is happening. *Recognize* requires developing the ability to notice, "deepening our perception to more effectively see and understand the pain we seek to address in the world" (Magee, 2019, p. 104). *Accept* means allowing the thoughts, emotions, and physical sensations occurring within us to exist for the moment, not trying to deny them, push them away, or judge them. Accepting does not mean passively resigning or that something cannot be changed in the future; rather it requires pausing long enough to clearly see and experience. The heart of the RAIN practice, *investigate* asks us to look compassionately and courageously into what is coming up in ourselves. We might ask: *Why am I feeling this way? What might this emotion be telling me?* Finally, *non-identify* involves enhancing our psychological flexibility by "learning to let go of tendencies to get stuck or to identify with the thoughts and emotions we uncover" in the RAIN process (Magee, 2019, p. 106). We remind ourselves that we are not our thoughts and emotions and avoid tunnel vision by remembering the spaciousness of the mind. School leaders can apply RAIN to their work using the following adapted practice:

Step 1: *Recognize*

As a school administrator, become aware of reactions in the body, even subtle ones, particularly as you interact with race, ethnicity, and gender in your school. For instance, when interacting with teachers of color, pay close attention to bodily sensations. Do you experience tension, tightness, or discomfort in your neck, shoulders, stomach, or other area? Likewise, when addressing issues of discipline, test scores, or access to resources with students of color or minority populations at the school, what happens in your body?

Step 2: *Accept*

Allow these reactions to occur without resistance. Don't fight them. Bring a compassionate, nonjudgmental attitude toward yourself, knowing you are giving yourself enough pause to transform this energy and make a positive change.

Step 3: Investigate

Meditate on the bodily sensations that have arisen within the context of race, inclusion, and equity. *Why am I feeling this way? Why is my body reacting this way, possibly having a stress response to this situation, to making this decision? What in my past, my race story, might be contributing to this reaction?*

Step 4: Non-Identify

Allow yourself to step back and observe your thoughts and bodily response. Understand that you are not this response, that you have the power—the flexibility of consciousness—to break this negative stress response. Consider what would be a more positive, inclusive response. Feel it in the body.

TONGLEN: ADVANCED MEDITATION FOR INCLUSIVE EDUCATIONAL LEADERSHIP

This advanced form of Buddhist meditation was intentionally saved for the end of the book. As Haberlin and Mette (2023) have posited, *tonglen*, sometimes called Atisha's Heart Meditation (after the originator), could hold promise for culturally responsive supervision. Tonglen is an age-old meditation practice, brought from India to Tibet in the eleventh century. The meditation requires imagining taking the suffering from others and substituting positivity, happiness, and well-being. While advanced, and sometimes problematic for practitioners, especially those new to meditation training, the practice uses radical imagination to dissolve barriers in the heart that cause us to feel separate from others. Tonglen is like weightlifting for the heart, building compassion and feelings of altruism by counteracting our habitual preoccupations and tendency to avoid suffering at the hands of oppressive systems in the United States, specifically that of other beings based on racial identity. Buddhist meditation teacher Pema Chödrön (2007) describes the practice this way: "In tonglen practice, we breathe in what we normally push away and send out what we normally cling to. This dissolves the ego's strategies and reveals the clarity of our mind" (p. 34). Tonglen meditation could help educational leaders explore their own experiences with diversity and inclusion and serve as a basis for them to engage in often-uncomfortable conversations around racial and social inequities. Figure 10.1 depicts the four stages of tonglen. This is followed by a detailed explanation of each stage as it can be situated within instructional supervision.

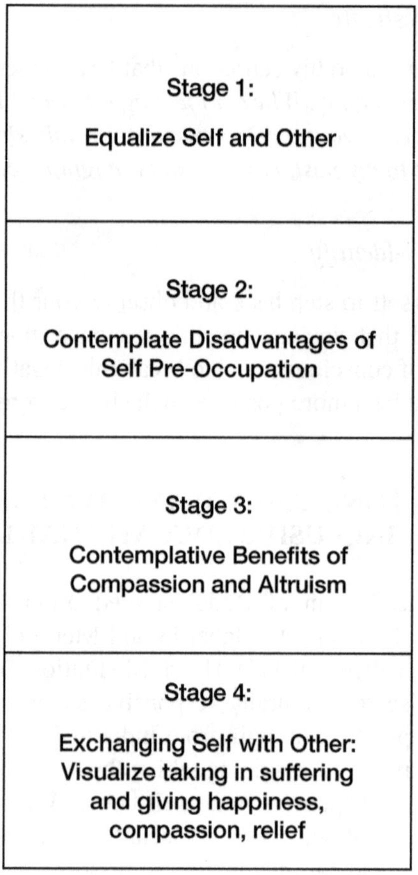

Figure 10.1.
Courtesy of author

> **Stage 1:**
> Equalize Self and Other
>
> **Stage 2:**
> Contemplate Disadvantages of Self Pre-Occupation
>
> **Stage 3:**
> Contemplative Benefits of Compassion and Altruism
>
> **Stage 4:**
> Exchanging Self with Other: Visualize taking in suffering and giving happiness, compassion, relief

Preparation for Tonglen

Before engaging in tonglen, consider the following suggestions: (1) Find a relatively quiet place, and (2) sit in a comfortable position either on a floor mat or chair. (3) The back should be straight but not stiff and the chin should be slightly tilted down, eyes either closed or looking downward. (4) Place the hands face up, cupped, below the waist, or face down, palms resting on the knees. (5) Begin focusing on the breath, simply observing the inhalation and exhalation through the nose. Do this for a minimum of 10 repetitions. *A final preparatory note: Tonglen is an intense meditation. If at any time during the process, it feels too heavy, elicits strong negative emotion, or even triggers trauma, simply stop the meditation. Bring your attention to your current experience using your senses of sight, sound, etc.*

Stage 1: Equalizing Self and Other Within the Context of Supervision

Reflect on how we create mental division and separation—for example, how various social constructs, such as race, ethnicity, nationality, socioeconomic status, and gender, create division and feelings of separateness. In educational leadership, consider how the experiences of students, including their race and socioeconomic status, create inequitable experiences and outcomes. Meditate more deeply on how your personal experiences—what you have read, discussed, and observed—might have created feelings of separation. As a child or student, how were you or classmates defined, labeled, or treated, perhaps being marginalized while progressing through K–12 education.

Reflect on the country's political system and process, on how it might have created polarizing views and stances. Contemplate how socially created gender roles regarding sexual orientation cause deeper divides. Further consider how your experience with socioeconomic status and race might have caused feelings of divisiveness. Finally, reflect on how educational leaders might unintentionally reinforce these mental divisions when working with teachers, staff, and students.

Stage 2: Detriments of Self-Preoccupation

During this stage, meditate on the underlying cause of feelings of separateness: the self-centered, preoccupation of the ego, or the "me, mine, I" principle (Neale, 2013). Contemplate how much time we spend thinking about our own interests, goals, and ambitions as educational leaders (What's in it for me?). Meditate on how this self-preoccupation can be a disservice to teachers, parents, students, and other stakeholders.

Stage 3: The Benefits of Compassion and Altruism

Now, shift and contemplate the advantages of being compassionate and altruistic. Remember a time when you experienced feeling love, happiness, success, or fulfillment and how others were connected or involved. Soak in the positive feelings experienced when helping another by being supportive and caring. Consider how our well-being is intertwined with others. Think of the emotional benefit that comes from being compassionate and altruistic within our roles as educational leaders.

Stage 4: Exchanging Self and Other

During the final stage of tonglen, you utilize radical imagining to experience firsthand the suffering of another. Mentally picture someone connected to your supervision role—a colleague, a teacher, a student—who might be experiencing discomfort, increased stress, or trauma. As you breathe in, imagine taking their negativity or suffering in the form of a thick, heavy fog that leaves them and comes into your nostrils and into your heart. Also, imagine the heart expanding, becoming like an ocean, and the negative energy simply a drop of water being easily and completely absorbed. As you breathe out, imagine that you are sending a beam of light toward their heart that contains support, compassion, and caring. After completing several rounds, keep the eyes closed for a minute or two, feeling the heart and body. When ready, open the eyes.

FINAL THOUGHTS ON MINDFULNESS-BASED SUPERVISION

As mentioned earlier in this book, mindfulness is not panacea for the problems of supervision. Embracing mindfulness will not suddenly gain the field more respect and bring it out of traveling incognito. Mindfulness will not solve the ongoing dilemma of whether supervision should include evaluation practices. What mindfulness can do is bring educational leaders—tasked with the all-important responsibility of preparing and coaching the country's teachers—more self-awareness, more awareness of those they impact, and help them operate from a place of centeredness rather than negative reactivity. Mindfulness can literally provide some breathing space, empowering school leaders with the chance to clear their minds, ground themselves, listen more deeply, and respond more wisely. Mindfulness is a psychological trait that can enhance every aspect of the supervisory process. Like a vitamin, it can supplement what is currently being done. A mindfulness-based approach to supervision is simply being more intentional about our practice, utilizing tools and methods to keep ourselves more in the present moment so we can be our best for those that need us most.

Resources

The following resources are for educational leaders and other educators interested in learning more about mindfulness, meditation, and other contemplative practices. (*Note:* This is by no means an exhaustive list but rather a good starting point for those interested in learning more about mindfulness and meditation.)

MINDFULNESS/MEDITATION BOOKS

The Power of Now by Eckhart Tolle
 A classic book on mindfulness and meditation, *The Power of Now* offers practical advice and exercises for beginners.

Mindfulness: An Eight-Week Plan for Finding Peace in a Frantic World by Mark Williams and Danny Penma
 This book offers a practical and accessible introduction to mindfulness meditation.

Full Catastrophe Living: Using the Wisdom of Your Body and Mind to Face Stress, Pain, and Illness by Jon Kabat-Zinn
 This book introduces the practice of mindfulness-based stress reduction (MBSR), a technique for managing stress and anxiety through meditation.

Wherever You Go, There You Are by Jon Kabat-Zinn
Zinn's book offers a practical guide to mindfulness meditation, with exercises and tips for integrating mindfulness into everyday life.

A Path With Heart by Jack Kornfield
Kornfield explores the intersection of mindfulness and spirituality, offering insights and guidance for those seeking a deeper connection to themselves and the world around them.

Real Happiness: The Power of Meditation by Sharon Salzberg
This book offers a practical guide to meditation, with exercises and guidance for developing a daily meditation practice.

Mindfulness in Plain English by Bhante Henepola Gunaratana
Readers receive a straightforward introduction to mindfulness meditation, with practical tips and exercises for beginners.

The Art of Power by Thich Nhat Hanh
Zen Master Hanh explores the relationship between mindfulness and power, offering guidance for developing inner strength and wisdom.

MINDFULNESS/MEDITATION WEBSITES

Mindful: https://www.mindful.org
A website dedicated to mindfulness and meditation, Mindful.org offers a variety of resources for beginners, including guided meditations, articles, and podcasts.

Tricycle: *The Buddhist Review*: https://tricycle.org
This online magazine covers all things Buddhism and meditation.

The Free Mindfulness Project: https://www.freemindfulness.org
This website provides "free access to mindfulness meditation exercises by inviting the wider mindfulness community to share their resources here."

Pocket Mindfulness: https://www.pocketmindfulness.com
Website started by Alfred James, father of two, with lots of user-friendly, free resources.

PROMINENT MINDFULNESS/MEDITATION TEACHERS

Jon Kabat-Zinn: https://jonkabat-zinn.com
Jack Kornfield: https://jackkornfield.com
Sharon Salzberg: https://www.sharonsalzberg.com
Joseph Goldstein: https://www.josephgoldstein.com
Pema Chödrön: https://pemachodronfoundation.org
Eckhart Tolle: https://eckharttolle.com
Tara Brach: https://www.tarabrach.com
Kristin Neff: https://self-compassion.org
Mark Williams: https://mindfulness.com/teacher/mark-williams
Miles Neale: https://www.milesneale.com

MINDFULNESS AND MEDITATION APPS

Headspace: One of the most popular mindfulness and meditation apps available, Headspace offers guided meditations for beginners and advanced practitioners alike.
Calm: Another popular meditation app, Calm offers guided meditations, sleep stories, and relaxation exercises.
Insight Timer: A free meditation app with over 100,000 guided meditations from a variety of teachers, as well as a timer for self-guided meditation.
The Mindfulness App: This app offers guided meditations for beginners, as well as tools to help you establish a daily mindfulness practice.

CENTERS FOR MINDFULNESS/MEDITATION/ CONTEMPLATIVE STUDIES

UCLA Mindful Awareness Research Center: https://www.uclahealth.org/programs/marc
Contemplative Studies Initiative & Concentration at Brown University: https://www.brown.edu/academics/contemplative-studies/
Mind-Body Wellness Program at the University of Vermont: https://www.uvm.edu/health/mindfulness
Center for Wellness & Health Promotion at Harvard University: https://wellness.huhs.harvard.edu
Center for Integrative Health & Wellness at Ohio State University: https://wexnermedical.osu.edu/integrative-health/resources/mindfulness-practices

MINDFULNESS PROGRAMS

Mindfulness-Based Stress Reduction: https://www.ummhealth.org/umass-memorial-medical-center/services-treatments/center-for-mindfulness/mindfulness-programs/mbsr-8-week-online-live

This evidence-based program was developed by Jon Kabat-Zinn and teaches mindfulness meditation as a way to reduce stress and improve overall health and well-being.

Penn Program for Mindfulness: https://www.pennmedicine.org/for-patients-and-visitors/find-a-program-or-service/mindfulness/program-offerings

This program "provides powerful tools for coping and personal growth. Combining modern cognitive science with ancient mindfulness techniques, the program teaches participants to change the way that they experience themselves and their world."

References

Alderfer, L. (2015). *Teaching from the heart of mindfulness*. Green Writers Press.

Allen, S. (2018). *The science of generosity* [white paper]. John Templeton Foundation by the Greater Good Science Center, UC Berkeley.

American Psychological Association (n.d.). *Gratitude*. https://dictionary.apa.org/gratitude.

Baylor, A. L. (1997). A three-component conception of intuition: Immediacy, sensing relationships, and reason. *New Ideas in Psychology, 15*(2), 185–94.

Barbezat, D. P. & Bush, M. (2013). *Contemplative practices in higher education: Powerful methods to transform teaching and learning*. John Wiley & Sons.

Blackwell, K. (2019). Race and the body: Why somatic practices are essential for racial justice. *The Arrow, 6*(1), 10–23.

Brown, K. W. & Ryan, R. M. (2003). The benefits of being present: Mindfulness and its role in psychological well-being. *Journal of Personality and Social Psychology, 84*(4), 822–48.

Brown, K. M. (2004). Leadership for social justice and equity: Weaving a transformative framework and pedagogy. *Educational Administration Quarterly, 40*, 77–108.

Bullock, S. M. (2007). Finding my way from teacher to teacher educator: Valuing innovative pedagogy and inquiry into practice. In T. Russell & J. Loughran (eds.), *Enacting a pedagogy of teacher education: Values, relationships and practices* (pp. 77–94). Routledge.

Burnham, J. F. (2001). *A study of North Carolina principal fellows' perceptions of the adequacy of their administrative training*. The University of North Carolina at Charlotte.

Burns, R. W. & Badiali, B. (2016a). Framing conceptual, procedural, and emotional support for supervisors. *Teacher Education and Practice, 29*(2), 397.

——— (2016b). Unearthing the complexities of clinical pedagogy in supervision: Identifying the pedagogical skills of supervisors. *Action in Teacher Education, 38*(2), 156–74.

Burns, R. W., Jacobs, J. & Yendol-Hoppey, D. (2019). A framework for naming the scope and nature of preservice teacher supervision in clinically based teacher preparation: Tasks, high-leverage practices, and pedagogical routines of practice. *The Teacher Educator*, 1–25. https://doi.org/10.1080/08878730.2019.1682091.

Clark, R., Anderson, N. B., Clark, V. R. & Williams, D. R. (1999). Racism as a stressor for African Americans: A biopsychosocial model. *American Psychologist*, *54*(10), 805.

Chödrön, P. (2007). *No time to lose: A timely guide to the way of the Bodhisattva.* Shambhala Publications.

Costa, A. & Garmston, R. (1989). The art of cognitive coaching: Supervision for intelligent teaching. *Training Syllabus, Institute for Intelligent Behavior*, 950.

Dane, E. & Pratt, M. G. (2009). Conceptualizing and measuring intuition: A review of recent trends. In G. P. Hodgkinson & J. K. Ford (eds.), *International review of industrial and organizational psychology*, vol. 24, 1–49. Wiley.

Dantley, M. E. (2005a). African American spirituality and Cornel West's notions of prophetic pragmatism: Restructuring educational leadership in American urban schools. *Educational Administration Quarterly, 41*, 651–74. doi:10.1177/0013161X04274274.

Dorman, E. H., Byrnes, K. & Dalton, J. E. (eds.) (2017). *Impacting teaching and learning: Contemplative practices, pedagogy, and research in education.* Rowman & Littlefield.

Dalton, J. E., Dorman, E. H. & Byrnes, K. (eds.) (2018). *The teaching self: Contemplative practices, pedagogy, and research in education.* Rowman & Littlefield.

de Quervain, D., et al. (2004). The neural basis of altruistic punishment. *Science, 305,* 1254–58. doi: 10.1126/science.1100735.

Dewey, J. (1929). *The quest for certainty.* GP Putnam's Sons.

Duncan, L. G., Coatsworth, J. D. & Greenberg, M. T. (2009). Pilot study to gauge acceptability of a mindfulness-based, family-focused preventive intervention. *The Journal of Primary Prevention, 30*(5) (at press).

Emmons, R. A. & McCullough, M. E. (2003). Counting blessings versus burdens: An experimental investigation of gratitude and subjective well-being in daily life. *Journal of Personality and Social Psychology, 84*(2), 377.

Fox, G. R., et al. (2015). Neural correlates of gratitude. *Frontiers in Psychology*, 1491.

Gay, G. & Kirkland, K. (2003). Developing cultural critical consciousness and self-reflection in preservice teacher education. *Theory Into Practice, 42*, 181–87. doi:10.1207/s15430421tip4203_3.

Glanz, J. (1991). *Bureaucracy and professionalism: The evolution of public school supervision.* Fairleigh Dickinson University Press.

——— (1997). The Tao of supervision: Taoist insights into the theory and practice of educational supervision. *Journal of Curriculum and Supervision, 12*(3), 193.

——— (2000). Supervision: Don't discount the value of the modern. In J. Glanz & L. S. Behar-Horenstein (eds.), *Paradigm debates in curriculum and supervision: Modern and postmodern perspectives* (pp. 70–92). Bergin & Garvey.

——— (2018). Chronicling perspectives about the state of instructional supervision by eight prominent scholars of supervision. *The Journal of Educational Supervision, 1*(1). https://doi.org/10.31045/jes.1.1.1.

——— (2021). Personal reflections on supervision as instructional leadership: From whence it came and to where shall it go? *Journal of Educational Supervision, 4*(3), 66.

Glickman, C. D. (1981). *Developmental supervision: Alternative practices for helping teachers improve instruction.* Association for Supervision and Curriculum Development.

——— (1992). *Supervision in transition: 1992 yearbook of the association for supervision and curriculum development.* Association for Supervision and Curriculum Development.

Glickman, C. & Burns, R. W. (2020). *Leadership for learning: How to bring out the best in every teacher.* ASCD.

Glickman, C. D., Gordon, S. P. & Ross-Gordon, J. M. (2017). *Supervision and instructional leadership: A developmental approach* (tenth ed.). Pearson.

Glickman, M. (2002). *Beyond the breath: Extraordinary mindfulness through whole-body Vipassana meditation.* Tuttle Publishing.

Goldhammer, R. (1969). *Clinical supervision: Special methods for the supervision of teachers.* Holt, Rinehart, and Winston.

Gordon, S. P. (1997). Has the field of supervision evolved to a point that it should be called something else? In J. Glanz & R. F. Neville (eds.), *Educational supervision: Perspectives, Issues, and Controversies.* Christopher-Gordon Pub.

——— (2019). Educational supervision: Reflections on its past, present, and future. *Journal of Educational Supervision, 2*(2), 27–52.

Greater Good Science Center (2023). *Gratitude journal.* https://ggia.berkeley.edu/practice/gratitude_journal.

Greene, M. (1973). *Teacher as stranger.* Wadsworth.

Grossman, P., et al. (2009). Teaching practice: A cross-professional perspective. *Teachers College Record, 111*(9), 2055–2100.

Grumet, M. (1979). Supervision and situation. *Journal of Curriculum Theorizing, 1*(1).

Haberlin, S. R. (2019). *Supervision in every breath: Enacting Zen in an elementary education teacher program* [unpublished doctoral dissertation]. University of South Florida.

Haberlin, S. & Mette, I. (2023). Exploring inclusive leadership through embodied mindfulness and compassion: A contemplative racial justice supervision framework. *Inclusive School Leadership.* Council of Professors of Instructional Supervision (book series).

Haberlin, S. (2023). Culturally responsive supervision and mindfulness: A somatic, embodied practice. In I. Mette, D. Cormier & Y. Oilveras-Ortiz (eds.), *Culturally responsive instructional supervision* (at press).

Hall, L. (2013). *Mindful coaching: How mindfulness can transform coaching practice.* Kogan Page Publishers.

Hanson, R. (2009). *Buddha's brain: The practical neuroscience of happiness, love and wisdom.* New Harbinger.

Hanushek, E. A., et al. (2019). The achievement gap fails to close. *Education Next, 19*(3), 8–17.

Hayes, S. C., et al. (2006). Acceptance and commitment therapy: Model, processes and outcomes. *Behaviour research and therapy, 44*(1), 1–25.

Hayes, J. A. & Vinca, M. (2017). Therapist presence, absence, and extraordinary presence. In *How and why are some therapists better than others? Understanding therapist effects* (pp. 85–99). American Psychological Association.

Helminski, K. E. (2017). *Living presence (revised): The Sufi path to mindfulness and the essential self.* Penguin.

Hosic, J. F. (1920). The democratization of supervision. *School and Society, 11*(4), 331–36.

Huberman, A. (2021). The science of gratitude and how to build a gratitude practice. https://hubermanlab.com/the-science-of-gratitude-and-how-to-build-a-gratitude-practice/.

Jans-Beken, L., et al. (2020). Gratitude and health: An updated review. *The Journal of Positive Psychology, 15*(6), 743–82.

Kabat-Zinn, J. (2013). *Full catastrophe living: how to cope with stress, pain and illness using mindfulness meditation* (revised ed.). Hachette UK.

——— (2005). *Coming to our senses: Healing ourselves and the world through mindfulness.* Hachette UK.

——— (2013). *Full catastrophe living: How to cope with stress, pain and illness using mindfulness meditation* (revised ed.). Hachette UK.

Kesier, D. (2018). If we teach who we are, who are we? In L. Jans-Beken et al. (2020). Gratitude and health: An updated review. *The Journal of Positive Psychology, 15*(6), 743–82.

Kessler, R. (2000). The teaching presence. *Virginia Journal of Education, 94*(2), 4.

Khalifa, M. (2011). Principal expectations and principal behavior: Responding to teacher acquiescence. *The Urban Review, 43*(5), 702–27.

——— (2020). *Culturally responsive school leadership* (fourth ed.). Harvard Education Press.

Khalifa, M. A., Gooden, M. A. & Davis, J. E. (2016). Culturally responsive school leadership: A synthesis of the literature. *Review of Educational Research, 86*(4), 1272–1311.

Kornfield, J. (2009). *The wise heart: A guide to the universal teachings of Buddhist psychology.* Bantam.

——— (2023). *Audio: Letting go meditation.* https://jackkornfield.com/letting-go-meditation/.

Korthagen, F. A., et al. (eds.) (2013). *Teaching and learning from within: A core reflection approach to quality and inspiration in education.* Routledge.

Livers, S. D., et al. (2022). The complexities and discourse of supervision for equity and justice in teaching and teacher education. *Journal of Educational Supervision, 5*(2), 1.

Magee, R. V. (2019). *The inner work of racial justice: Healing ourselves and transforming our communities through mindfulness.* TarcherPerigee.

Marzano, R. J., Frontier, T. & Livingston, D. (2011). *Effective supervision: Supporting the art and science of teaching.* ASCD.

MasterClass (2022). Beginner's mind: How to develop a beginner's mind. https://www.masterclass.com/articles/beginners-mind.

Mayer, J. D., Caruso, D. R. & Salovey, P. (1997). Emotional intelligence meets traditional standards for an intelligence. *Intelligence, 27*(4), 267–98.

McCullough, M. E., Emmons, R. A. & Tsang, J. A. (2002). The grateful disposition: A conceptual and empirical topography. *Journal of Personality and Social Psychology, 82*(1), 112–27.

McGregor, D. (1960). Theory x and theory y. *Organization Theory, 358*(374), 5.

McKenzie, K. B., et al. (2008). From the field: A proposal for educating leaders for social justice. *Educational Administration Quarterly, 44*, 111–38. doi:10.1177/0013161X07309470.

McNaughton, R. D. (2003). *The use of meditation and intuition in decision-making: Reports from executive meditators* [unpublished doctoral dissertation]. Fielding Graduate Institute.

Meade, E. (2019). The history and origin of meditation. https://positivepsychology.com/history-of-meditation/.

Melnechenko, K. L. (2003, April). To make a difference: Nursing presence. *Nursing Forum, 38*(2), 18. Blackwell Publishing Ltd.

Mette, I. M., et al. (2017). The wicked problem of the intersection between supervision and evaluation. *International Electronic Journal of Elementary Education, 9*(3), 709–24.

Mette, I. M. (2020). Reflections on supervision in the time of COVID-19. *Journal of Educational Supervision, 3*(3), 1–6. https://doi.org/10.31045/jes.3.3.1.

Mette, I. M., Aguilar, I. & Wieczorek, D. (2020). *A fifty state review of teacher supervision and evaluation systems: The influence of ESSA and implications for policy and practice.* Paper session at the Annual Meeting of the American Educational Research Association, San Francisco, CA.

Miller, J. P. & Nigh, K. (eds.) (2017). *Holistic education and embodied learning.* IAP.

Mingyur Rinpoche, Y. (2007). *The joy of living.* Harmony Books.

Murphy, M. P. (2017). *Conducting effective pre-observation conferences for teacher growth.*

Neff, K. (2003). Self-compassion: An alternative conceptualization of a healthy attitude toward oneself. *Self and Identity, 2*(2), 85–101.

Noddings, N. (2013). *Caring: A relational approach to ethics and moral education.* University of California Press.

Nolan, J. & Hoover, L. A. (2011). *Teacher supervision and evaluation: Theory into practice* (third ed.). Wiley.

Ottati, V., et al. (2015). When self-perceptions of expertise increase closed-minded cognition: The earned dogmatism effect. *Journal of Experimental Social Psychology, 61*, 131–38.

Owens, L. R. (2020). *Love and rage: The path of liberation through anger*. North Atlantic Books.

Pajak, E. (2000). *Approaches to clinical supervision*. Christopher-Gordon Pub.

—— (2003). *Honoring diverse teaching styles: A guide for supervisors*. Association for Supervision and Curriculum Development.

Payne, C. M. (2008). *So much reform, so little change: The persistence of failure in urban schools*. Harvard Education Press.

Remmers, C., Topolinski, S. & Michalak, J. (2015). Mindful intuition: Does mindfulness influence the access to intuitive processes? *The Journal of Positive Psychology, 10*(3), 282–92.

Richards, K., Campenni, C. & Muse-Burke, J. (2010). Self-care and well-being in mental health professionals: The mediating effects of self-awareness and mindfulness. *Journal of Mental Health Counseling, 32*(3), 247–64.

Rodgers, C. R. & Raider-Roth, M. B. (2006). Presence in teaching. Teachers and Teaching: *Theory and Practice, 12*(3), 265–87.

Runcan, P. (2013). *Supervision in educational, social and medical services professions*. Cambridge Scholars Publishing.

Sadler-Smith, E. (2007). *Inside intuition*. Routledge.

—— (2010). *The intuitive mind: Profiting from the power of your sixth sense*. John Wiley & Sons.

Schnitker, S. A. (2012). An examination of patience and well-being. *The Journal of Positive Psychology, 7*(4), 263–80.

Schnitker, S. A. & Emmons, R. A. (2007). Patience as a virtue: Religious and psychological perspectives. *Research in the Social Scientific Study of Religion, 18*, 177–207. https://doi.org/10.1163/ej.9789004158511.i-301.69.

Seligman, M. E. P., et al. (2005). Positive psychology progress: Empirical validation of interventions. *American Psychologist, 60*, 410–21.

Seligman, M. E. (2011). *Flourish: A visionary new understanding of happiness and well-being*. Simon and Schuster.

Sergiovanni, T. J. & Starratt, R. J. (2007). *Supervision: A redefinition* (eighth ed.). McGraw Hill.

Shumsky, S. (2001). *Exploring meditation: Master the ancient art of relaxation and enlightenment*. Red Wheel/Weiser.

Siegel, D. J. (2010). *Mindsight: The new science of personal transformation*. Bantam.

Silsbee, D. (2016). Developing resilience. In A. J. Viera & R. Kramer (eds.), *Management and leadership skills for medical faculty* (pp. 53–61). Springer, Cham.

—— (2010). *The mindful coach: Seven roles for facilitating leader development*. John Wiley & Sons.

Smith, L. (2021). How to be more patient. https://www.webmd.com/balance/features/how-to-be-more-patient#091e9c5e82224f04 (1–5).

Stanovich, K. E. & West, R. F. (2008). On the relative independence of thinking biases and cognitive ability. *Journal of Personality and Social Psychology, 94*(4), 672.

Sullivan, S. & Glanz, J. (2005). *Supervision that improves teaching: Strategies and techniques*. Corwin Press.

Sullivan, S. (2004). Changing context of supervision. https://www.corwin.com/sites/default/files/upm-binaries/6652_sullivan_ch_1.pdf.
Swain, J. E., et al. (2012). Parenting and beyond: Common neurocircuits underlying parental and altruistic caregiving. *Parenting, 12*(2–3), 115–123. https://doi.org/10.1080/15295192.2012.680409.
Tang, Y. Y., et al. (2010). Short-term meditation induces white matter changes in the anterior cingulate. *Proceedings of the National Academy of Sciences, 107*(35), 15649–652.
Villate & Butand (2017). Cultivating mindful teachers: Using a mindfulness-based teaching approach with student teachers. In E. H. Dorman, K. Byrnes & J. E. Dalton (eds.), *Impacting teaching and learning: Contemplative practices, pedagogy, and research in education*. Rowman & Littlefield.
Vipassana Research Institute (n.d.). What is Vipassana? https://www.vridhamma.org/What-is-Vipassana.
Waite, D. (1995). Teacher resistance in a supervision conference. *Discourse and Power in Educational Organizations*, 71–87.
Watson, K. T. (2019). *Revealing and uprooting cellular violence: Black men and the biopsychosocial impact of racial microaggressions*. ProQuest LLC.
Wells, C. M. (2013). Principals responding to constant pressure: Finding a source of stress management. *NASSP Bulletin, 97*(4), 335–49.
Wheeler, J. A., Gorey, K. M. & Greenblatt, B. (1998). The beneficial effects of volunteering for older volunteers and the people they serve: a meta-analysis. *The International Journal of Aging and Human Development, 47*(1), 69–79. https://doi.org/10.2190/VUMP-XCMF-FQYU-V0JH.
Williams, J., Ritter, J. & Bullock, S. M. (2012). Understanding the complexity of becoming a teacher educator: Experience, belonging, and practice within a professional learning community. *Studying Teacher Education, 8*(3), 245–60.
Williams, R. (2018). 5 meditation styles for beginners: Choosing the right type for you. https://chopra.com/articles/5-meditation-styles-for-beginners-choosing-the-right-type-for-you.
Wood, A. M., Froh, J. J. & Geraghty, A. W. (2010). Gratitude and well-being: A review and theoretical integration. *Clinical Psychology Review*, 30(7), 890–905.
Zedelius, C. M. & Schooler, J. W. (2015). Mind wandering "ahas" versus mindful reasoning: Alternative routes to creative solutions. *Frontiers in Psychology, 6*, 834.
Zyblock, D. M. (2010, April). Nursing presence in contemporary nursing practice. In *Nursing Forum, 45*(2), 120–24. Blackwell Publishing Inc.

Index

acceptance, 38, 89; in the clinical supervision cycle, 12, 83–85; cultivating acceptance, mindfulness-based strategies for, 85–86, 91; in educational supervision, 82–83; as a mindfulness attitude, 10, 81, 83, 95, 96
acknowledging, technique of, 85
action research model, 49
altruism, 101, *102,* 103
anxiety, 6, 77, 82, 93, 105

Badiali, Bernard, 26
Barbezat, Daniel P., 45
Baylor, Amy L., 60
beginner's mind, 47, 54; in the clinical supervision cycle, 49–50, 55, 76, 96; educational supervision and, 48–49; as a mindfulness attitude, 9, 10, 11, 82, 95
Bell Exercise, 64–65
Blackwell, Kelsey, 97–98
the body: bias and the body, 97–98; body awareness, 31, 70; body scan meditation, 7, 67–68, 99
Brach, Tara, 34, 107
the brain, 6–7, 88, 97
breath, *33,* 57, 69, 80, 98; breath meditation, 7, 9, 34, 52, 69, 77–78, 92; gratitude practice and focus on the breath, 89, 92; mala beads, breathwork done with, 65–67, 70; mindful breathing, 4, 23–26, 28, 31, 42, 51, 82, 99; observing the breath, 51, 68, 79, 94; simple breath awareness, 9–10; in the Stage Exercise, 44–45; Three-Minute Breathing Space, 43, 51, 55; in *tonglen* practice, 102, 104
Brown, Kathleen M., 61
Buddhism, 5, 37, 44, 71, 97, 106; the Buddha, 3, *30,* 34, 75; loving-kindness meditation, 31, 68–69; mindfulness concept as rooted in, 2–3; *tonglen* as an advanced Buddhist method, 101–4; Vipassana practice, 9–10, 34; Zen Buddhism, 30, 47–48, 52, 72, 106
Burnham, Judith F., 16
Burns, Rebecca W., 26
Bush, Mirabai, 45

CARE for Teachers program, 44
Chögyam Trungpa Rinpoche, 5
choice, 1, 2, 5, 9, *33,* 68
classroom observation stage, 68, 86; acceptance and non-judgment, developing, 84–85; beginner's mind,

infusing with, 48, 49–50, 51, *52,* 53, 55–56; in the clinical supervision model, 21, 22–23, *24,* 40; gratitude and generosity, cultivating, 90, 94; letting go and non-striving during, 76, 80; patience and trust, displaying, 62–63, 70; presence, cultivating, 39, 40
clinical supervision model, *17,* 19, 58, 76; acceptance and non-judgment, exhibiting, 83–85; beginner's mind, developing, 49–50; describing and defining, 20–22; gratitude and generosity, fostering, 89–90; mindfulness, converging with, 22–26; patience and trust in, 62–63; presence, role of, 39–40
Cogan, Morris, 21
cognitive coaching, 18, *19*
conditioning, 1, 98
Council of Professors of Supervision (COPIS), 20
COVID-19 pandemic, 19
critical consciousness, 96
critical self-reflection, 20, 96–97

Dane, Erik, 61
deep listening, 11, 37–38, *40,* 45, 95
Dewey, John, 18
"don't know" mind, 53–54, 55

educational platform, crafting, 74–75
Eightfold Path, 3
equity, 13, 19, 101

feedback, 21, *27,* 39, 41, 45, 77, 89, 93; post-conference feedback, 22, *23, 24, 63, 84,* 90; supervision backpack and, 74, *75*; trust, feedback in a space of, 46, 59
Four Noble Truths, 3

generosity: in the clinical cycle, 89–90, 93–94; happiness as linked with, 88–89; as a mindfulness attitude, 10, 12–13, 96; mindfulness-based strategies to cultivate generosity, 91–93
Glanz, Jeffrey, 16, 18
Glickman, Carl D., 18, *19,* 20, 58
Glickman, Marshall, 34
Goenka, Satya Narayana, 34
Goldhammer, Robert, 21
Goldstein, Joseph, 92, 107
Gordon, Stephen P., 20–21
gratitude: in the clinical cycle, 89–90, 93–94; gratitude journals, 86, 87–88, 91–92; as a mindfulness attitude, 10, 12–13, 96
grounding, *24, 25,* 93; breathwork and grounding, 43; mindfulness, grounding in, 44, 104; in the Stage Exercise, 45

Haberlin, Steve, 101
Hall, Liz, 7, 32, 42, 43
Hazi, Helen M., 20
Helminski, Kabir E., 37
Hosic, James F., 18

ignoring, 26, *27,* 41, 50, 64, 77
immediate response skills, 26, *27,* 40–41, 50, 63–64, 77
inclusion, 13, 101
insight, 3, 34, 50, *52,* 56, 80, 98; insight resources, 34, 107; intuition and insight, 59–60; mindfulness, insight from, 1, 5
intention and attachment matrix, 73
intervening, 26, *27,* 41, 64
intuition, *24,* 64, 97; body scan meditation to tap into, 67, 68; in clinical supervision cycle, 62–63, 69–70, 76; trust, as linked with, 12, 57, 59–61

Journal of Educational Supervision, 8, 20
journals and journaling, 86, 87–88, 91–92, 93
Jung, Carl, 62

Kabat-Zinn, Jon, 47, 57, 63; MBSR, establishing, 5, 105, 108; on meditation, 34, 59; as a mindfulness teacher, 61, 72, 89, 106, 107
Keiser, David L., 44–45
Kessler, Rachael, 38
Khalifa, Muhammad A., 96
Koestler, Arthur, 59–60
Kornfield, Jack, 34, 53, 72, 78, 92, 106, 107

Lao Tzu, 71
Lazar, Sara W., 6
leadership, 20, 38; awareness-based leadership, 2, 13; meditation, recalling leadership role during, 85–86; mindfulness for school leaders, 8, 10; patience needed for leaders, 63–64; six response skills of leaders, 40–41, 50; *tonglen* practice for inclusive educational leadership, 101–4
letting go, 71, 75; in the clinical supervision cycle, 12, 76, 79–80; in educational supervision, 74, 79–80; goals, approaching with an attitude of, 72–73; letting go meditation, 78–79; as a mindfulness attitude, 10, 96; mindfulness-based practices for letting go, 77–79
Lindsay, Emily K., 81
Livers, Stefanie D., 19
loving-kindness, 31, 68–69

Magee, Rhonda V., 99
Maharishi Mahesh Yogi, 5
mala bead bracelets, 65–67, 70
mantras, 30, *33,* 65, 66, 78
Marzano, Robert J., 20
McNaughton, 61
meals, mindful practice during, 54–55
meditation, *33,* 57, 96; acceptance in meditation practice, 81–82, 85–86; body scan meditation, 7, 67–68, 99; breath meditation, 7, 9, 34, 52, 77–78, 92; in Buddhist tradition, 2–3, *30;* "don't know" mind meditation, 53–54; four foundations of mindfulness, meditative pedagogy of, 3–5; gratitude meditation, 91, 92; guided meditations, 4, 28n1, 34; letting go meditation, 78–79; loving-kindness meditation, 31, 68–69; mala beads as used for, 65–67; meditation bell exercise, 64–65; meditation cushions, 26, 32; meditation resources, 105–8; mindfulness meditation, 6–7, 8, 29, 31, 32, 58, 59, 61, 98, 99–100; sitting meditation, 51, 65, 67, 72, 78–79, 85, 89, 92; stress, meditation as relieving, 30, 32, 34, 77; *tonglen* as advanced meditation, 101–4; Transcendental Meditation, 5, 30; Vipassana meditation, 9–10, 34
Mette, Ian M., 96, 101
Miller, John, P., 38
Mindful Minute, 42–43, 51, 52, 55, 56
mindfulness, 40, 47, 82, 89; acceptance and non-judgment, cultivating, 12, 81–86; beginner's mind, mindfulness-based strategies to cultivate, 51–55; body scan mindfulness practice, 7, 67–68, 98; choosing a mindfulness meditation method, 11, 31; clinical supervision cycle, converging with mindfulness, 22–25; defining and describing mindfulness, 1–2; educational leaders, mindfulness resources for, 105–8; educational supervision, relevance of mindfulness to, 8–9; embodied mindfulness and self-reflection, 96–97; four foundations of mindfulness, 3–5, 23, 26, 78; gratitude and generosity, cultivating with mindfulness, 89, 91–93; immediate response skills, mindfulness enhancing, 26, *28;* intuition, as strengthening,

61–62; letting go, mindfulness-based practices for, 71–72, 77–79; mindful attitude practice, examples of, *49, 76, 84, 90*; mindfulness-based supervision, 11, 13, 16, 104; mindfulness meditation, 6–7, 8, 29, 31, 32, 58, 59, 61, 98, 99–100; mindfulness moments, 9–10, 26–27, 41–42, 51; nine attitudes of mindfulness, 10, 37; patience and trust, developing with, 12, 57, 59, 64–69; presence, mindfulness-based practices to enhance, 42–46; supervision, mindfulness in the field of, 20–22, 26, 95, 98–101; Vipassana as a mindfulness practice, 9–10, 34
mindfulness-based stress reduction (MBSR), 5, 6, 105, 108
Murphy, Mark P., 8

Naropa University, 5, 44
Neale, Miles, 4–5, 28n1, 107
Nigh, Kelli, 38
Noddings, Nel, 38
nonattachment, 12, 73
non-judgment: in the clinical supervision cycle, 12, 83–85; in educational supervision, 82–83; as a mindfulness attitude, 1, 9, 10, 81, 83, 95, 96; mindfulness-based strategies for the cultivation of, 85–86, 91
non-striving, 10, 77; in the clinical supervision cycle, 76; educational supervision, non-striving in, 12, 74, 79–80; Taoist non-striving, 71
noticing, 43, *52,* 70, 84, 99; the breath, taking note of, 42, 51, 68; in the clinical supervision cycle, *24, 25, 40*; as an immediate response skill, 26, *27,* 41, 50, 63–64, 77; in mindfulness-based gratitude, 12–13; in the third foundation, 4–5

observation. *See* classroom observation stage

Pajak, Edward, 22, 62
patience: as an attitude of mindfulness, 9, 10, 57, 96; in the clinical supervision cycle, 11–12, 62–63, 69–70, 83, 84; in educational supervision, 58–59; mindfulness-based practices to encourage, 64–69
Pema Chödrön, 101, 107
PERMA Model, 87
pointing, 26, *27,* 41
post-conference stage of supervision, 9, 15, 44, 85; beginner's mind as informing, *49,* 50, 51, 56; in the clinical supervision model, 21, 22–23, 40; gratitude and generosity, cultivating, 90, 94; letting go and non-striving during, 76, 79–80; Mindful Minute, utilizing, 42–43; patience and trust, displaying, *63,* 70; presence, cultivating, 39, 40
Pratt, Michael G., 61
pre-conference stage of supervision, 15, *25,* 44, 56; acceptance and non-judgment, developing, 83, *84,* 86; beginner's mind as informing, 49, 51, 55; in the clinical supervision model, 21, 22–23; gratitude and generosity, cultivating, 89–90, 93–94; letting go and non-striving during, 76, 79; Mindful Minute, engaging in prior to meeting, 42–43; patience and trust, displaying, 62, *63,* 69–70; presence, cultivating, 39, *40*
presence, 81, 93; in the clinical supervision cycle, 11, 39–40; deep listening in the practice of, 37–38; educational supervision, presence in, 38–39; leadership, presence in, 40–41; as a mindfulness attitude, 95, 96; mindfulness-based practices to develop presence, 42–46
principals, 15, 19, 21, 38, 70, 77, 96; acceptance and non-judgment, cultivating, 12, 83; beginner's mind, using approach of, 48, 55; the

earliest principals, 16, *17*; gratitude, taking time for, 92, 93; intuition, allowing for, 60, 61, 64; Mindful Minute, practicing, 56; mindfulness as helpful for, 8, 9, 20, 98; pre- and post-conference activities, 69–70, 79–80, 94; Three-Minute Breathing Space, utilizing, 43

processing, 26, *27,* 41

professional development, 15–16

prosocial behavior, 87, 88

racism, 57, 95, 101; defining, 96–97; racial justice, 98, 99; self-examination on, 100

Raider-Roth, Miriam B., 38

RAIN method, 100–101

reactivity, 23, 84; habitual reactive tendencies, 4, *24, 25,* 98; increasing awareness of, *27, 33*; negative reactivity, 2, 9, 104; non-reactivity, 1, 81; stress reactivity, 3, 82

recognition, 1, 9

relaxed awareness, 42

reorientation grounding technique, 44

Rodgers, Carol R., 38

Ryan, Richard M., 61

Salzberg, Sharon, 1, 106, 107

Schnitker, Sarah A., 57

self-reflection, 20, 96–97

Seligman, Martin E. P., 87

Sergiovanni, Thomas J., 20–21, 74

Stage Exercise, 44–45

Starratt, Robert J., 20–21, 74

stress, 3, 12, 67, 70, 73, 81, 99, 101, 104; implicit bias and the stress response, 97; judgment, stress associated with, 82, 85; meditation as relieving, 30, 32, 34, 77; mindfulness-based stress reduction, 5, 6, 105, 108; permission to de-stress, 89; teachers, stress levels of, 8, 41

student learning outcomes, 22, *27,* 39, *52,* 63, 80

suffering, 3, 5, 57, 100, 101, *102,* 103–4

supervision, 13, 69, 73, 103; acceptance and non-judgment in, 12, 81, 82–83; beginner's mind, approaching with, 11, 47, 48–49, 51–55, 96; culturally responsive supervision, 98–101; current state of supervision, 19–20; defining and describing, 15–16; developmental model of supervision, 18, *19,* 20–21, 38–39, 58; directive supervision, 59, 70; evolving views of, 18–19; gratitude and generosity in, 12–13, 89; historical snapshot of, 16–17; intuition and, 61–62; letting go and non-striving as a supervisor, 12, 74–75, 78–80; mindful supervision, 8–9, 20, 29, 65–68, 85–86, 91–93, 95, 104; patience and trust in, 11–12, 58–59; presence in supervision, 11, 37, 38–39, 42–46. *See also* clinical supervision model

Suzuki, Shunryū, 47

Taoism, *30,* 71

Tao Te Ching (Lao Tzu), 71

Taylor, Fredrick, 16

teachable moments, 43, 44, 48, 60; beginner's mind as aiding in finding, 48, 50, 53; in classroom observation framework, 40, 62, *63,* 70, 79–80, 90, 94; ignoring as a tool, 50, 64, 77; immediate response skills and, 26, *27*; noticing, in the context of, 41, 50, 63–64, 77, 84–85; in post-conference situations, 80, 94

teacher inquiry model, 49

Thorndike, Edward, 16

tonglen (Atisha's Heart Meditation), 101–4

Transcendental Meditation, 5

trust, 46, 58; as an attitude of mindfulness, 9, 10, 57, 96; in the clinical supervision cycle, 11–12,

62–63, 69–70, 74; immediate response skills and, 63–64; intuition and trust as linked, 12, 57, 59–61; mindfulness-based practices to encourage trust, 64–69

two minds theory, 60–61

unpacking, 26, *27*, 41, 46

Vipassana meditation, 9–10, 34

wu wei (least action), 71

yoga, *30*, 31, 32

Zen Buddhism, 30, 47–48, 52, 72, 106

About the Author

Steve Haberlin, PhD (University of South Florida), is assistant professor of curriculum and instruction in the College of Community Innovation and Education at the University of Central Florida. His scholarship centers on the use of mindfulness and meditation within educational settings. He is also the author of *Meditation in the College Classroom: A Pedagogical Tool to Help Students De-Stress, Focus, and Connect* (Rowman & Littlefield).

www.ingramcontent.com/pod-product-compliance
Lightning Source LLC
Chambersburg PA
CBHW050244170426
43202CB00015B/2910